gerard manley hopkins

The Christian Critic Series

GERARD MANLEY HOPKINS

Edited by
JAMES F. SCOTT
CAROLYN D. SCOTT

Contributors
J. HILLIS MILLER
MARJORIE C. DOWNING
M. B. McNAMEE, S.J.
WILLIAM D. TEMPLEMAN
MARGARET R. STOBIE
ELGIN W. MELLOWN

B. HERDER BOOK CO.
314 NORTH JEFFERSON
ST. LOUIS, MISSOURI 63103

The Christian Critic Series is under the general editorship of Harry J. Cargas, Director of the Foreign Student Program, Saint Louis University.

820.9

of the Deutschland," is organized according to the scheme of meditation in Loyola's Spiritual Exercises. The next two articles address themselves to Hopkins' aesthetic, enjoying poetic traditions and influence which simultaneously inspired and challenged him. William Templeman present a valuable to explore similarities between Hopkins

FOREWORD

This anthology consists of six essays devoted to special topics in criticism of the poetry of Gerard Manley Hopkins. In making our selection from articles previously published in critical journals, we have endeavored to collect research which might provide students, scholars, and teachers with a reliable introduction to the poet, works which would place him in some appropriate philosophical and literary milieu. This seems particularly necessary in the case of a figure whose poetry and personality even the experienced reader often finds terribly elusive. Hence the logic of our choice and arrangement: a set of closely related studies designed to identify Hopkins through the influences which shaped him and the impression he himself made upon others.

What loyalties are crucial to the personal life of this Victorian-modern? What forces conditioned his intellectual and artistic development? J. Hillis Miller's essay seems ideally suited to provide a general orientation to these problems, touching as it does upon the uniqueness of Hopkins' mentality and the manner in which this temperament affects his approach to nature, art, and the godhead. Assessing "the creation of the self in Gerard Manley Hopkins," this introductory statement anticipates many matters of the poet's psychic formation which other contributors to the volume have investigated in a more specialized way. Marjorie Downing and Maurice McNamee present in their studies two crucial intellectual influences upon Hopkins—Duns Scotus and Ignatius Loyola, respectively. The burden of Miss Downing's argument is to demonstrate that Hopkins' favorite concepts, "inscape" and "instress," take on added meaning in the light of Scotus' theories of individuation and perception. Father McNamee, on the other hand, explains how "The Wreck of the Deutschland" is organized according to the scheme of meditation in Loyola's *Spiritual Exercises*. The next two articles address themselves to Hopkins' aesthetic, isolating poetic traditions of his own age which simultaneously inspired and challenged him. William Templeman proves it valuable to explore similarities between Hopkins and Whitman, and Margaret Stobie persuasively specifies the value of keeping in mind Hopkins' closeness to the minor Victorian poet Coventry Patmore. These two essays, of course, do not deny Hopkins' modernity, but simply offer a point of reference for discussion of his prosodic experiments and innovations. The last article in this collection is Elgin Mellown's study of Hopkins' reputation, an effort which complements the other essays through its attention to the image of himself Hopkins transmitted to later generations.

We have made no effort here to exhaust the investigation of sources influencing Hopkins (Keats and Newman are other influences that immediately come to mind), or to suggest that these should take priority over all others. Much less have we tried to represent all the critical methods applied to Hopkins' work, for such an undertaking, however valuable, obviously is beyond the scope of so slim a volume. Our bibliography is intended to give some indication of the range of recent scholarly concern, thus opening up to the reader other areas of inquiry. If the anthology succeeds in this it will fulfill our basic intention, which was to encourage new approaches to Hopkins, not canonize old ones.

James F. Scott
Carolyn D. Scott
St. Louis, Missouri

ACKNOWLEDGEMENTS

J. Hillis Miller, "The Creation of the Self in Gerard Manley Hopkins," *ELH*, XXII (December, 1955), 293-319. Reprinted by permission of The Johns Hopkins Press and the author.

Marjorie Downing, "Inscape and Instress: Further Analogies with Scotus," *PMLA*, LXV (March, 1950), 66-74. Reprinted by permission of The Modern Language Association and the author.

Maurice B. McNamee, S.J., "Mastery and Mercy in 'The Wreck of the Deutschland,'" *College English*, XXIII (January, 1962), 267-76. Reprinted with the permission of the National Council of Teachers of English and the author.

William D. Templeman, "Hopkins and Whitman: Evidence of Influence and Echoes," *Philological Quarterly*, XXXIII (January, 1954), 48-65. Reprinted by permission of the State University of Iowa Press and the author.

Margaret Stobie, "Patmore's Theory and Hopkins' Practice," *University of Toronto Quarterly*, XIX (October, 1949), 64-80. Reprinted by permission of the University of Toronto Press and the author.

Elgin W. Mellown, "The Reception of Gerard Manley Hopkins' Poetry, 1889-1930." This essay is a condensation by the author of two articles, "Gerard Manley Hopkins and His Public, 1889-1918," *Modern Philology*, LVII (November, 1959), 94-99; and "The Reception of Gerard Manley Hopkins' *Poems*, 1918-1930," *Modern Philology*, LXIII (August, 1965), 38-51. Reprinted and condensed with permission of the University of Chicago Press and the author.

Contents

Contents

J. Hillis Miller

THE CREATION OF THE SELF IN

GERARD MANLEY HOPKINS

Seen from one point of view Hopkins' work is some dozen nearly perfect lyrics. Seen from another perspective it is a heterogeneous collection of documents: poems, fragments of poems, letters, notebooks, undergraduate papers, lecture notes, incomplete commentaries, sermons, and so on. But within this seemingly chaotic mass we can detect a certain persistent structure. It is not a structure of abstract thought, nor is it a pattern of concrete images. To create this structure the world of sense perception has been transformed, through its verbalization, into the very substance of thought, and, one may say, into the very substance of Hopkins himself. This paper has as its limited objective the attempt to reveal this pervasive imaginative structure. One of its chief limitations is the necessity of describing discursively and seriatim what is really the nontemporal interior world of Hopkins, the total context in which any single poem exists and has its real meaning.

I

"I find myself both as man and as myself something most determined and distinctive, at pitch, more distinctive and higher pitched than anything I see." [1]

It would seem that the problem of individuation is solved for Hopkins with his first awareness of himself. No one has had a more intense apprehension of the uniqueness and substantiality of his own identity. Hopkins' version of the Descartean *Cogito* is: "I taste myself, therefore I exist." "My selfbeing," says Hopkins, "my consciousness and feeling of myself, that taste of myself, of I and me above and in all things . . . is more distinctive than the taste of ale or alum, more distinctive than the smell of walnutleaf or camphor, and is incommunicable by any means to another man (as when I was a child I used to ask myself: What must it be to be someone else?)." [2]

The self for Hopkins, in the very first moment in which it recognizes itself, recognizes itself not as a lack, an appeal, but as a plenitude. It does not need to seek something outside of itself as a source of its life, because that life has already been given. One finds oneself, from the beginning, a "throng and stack of being, so rich, so distinctive." [3] No one could be less like Mallarmé, for whom the moment of self-consciousness was the moment of a paralyzing sense of emptiness. Nor does self-awareness for Hopkins depend, as it does in the long tradition coming down from Locke, on sense perception of the external world. Much less does it depend on a relation to that world. No, Hopkins' *Cogito* is neither a purely intellectual self-consciousness arrived at by putting in doubt and separating from oneself everything which seems to come from the outside, nor is it the Lockean self-awareness which springs out of psychological nothingness in the moment of sensation. It is, like the first, entirely interior, entirely independent of the exterior world, since, for Hopkins, "when I compare myself, my being myself, with anything else whatever all things alike, all in the same degree, rebuff me with blank unlikeness; so that my knowledge of it, which is so intense, is from itself alone." [4]

The first moment of self-awareness is, then, not a thought, but a deeply organic sense experience which permeates the whole being, as in the famous formula of Condillac: "I am odor of rose." But it is a "taste of *oneself*," not of anything whatsoever which comes from the outside: "The development, refinement, condensation of nothing shows any sign of being able to match this to me or give me another taste of it, a taste even resembling it." [5] The self is already fully existent as soon as one is aware of oneself at all, and seems to form an eternally subsisting tasting of oneself which prolongs itself from moment to moment as long as one endures. Since it remains exactly the same through time, it is apparently indestructible. If it extends beyond disembodied consciousness, it is only to include a minimal sense of one's incarnation, minimal because it is a sense of incarnation in a simple, spaceless body which is wholly undifferentiated, wholly made up of a single taste.

The Hopkinsian self is, then, positive and definite, and it is vividly sensed, in the same way that objects in the exterior world are sensed. Intrinsic identity is a primary datum for man. He does not need to do anything at all to come into existence or to guarantee himself continued existence. And this intense possession of the sensation of self is the occasion of an elated joy at one's interior richness and at one's independence. If Hopkins' "taste of myself" reminds one of Sartre's "nausea," it is more because of the striking difference than because of the similarity. Sartre's nausea is disgust at the deeply organic sense of one's contingency, of the fact that one is not a free spirit, but is trapped in the flesh and enmeshed in a world of meaningless things. What is in Sartre a sickening sense of one's imprisonment in one's own unjustifiable material form is in Hopkins cause for rejoicing. For Hopkins the fact that "human nature" is "more highly pitched, selved, and distinctive than anything in the world" is proof that man is "life's pride and cared-for crown." [6] Man is, it seems, sufficient unto himself, like God.

But beneath the rejoicing in Hopkins at the uniqueness and self-subsistence of each human individual there is another current of thought, a current of wonder at this uniqueness, a wonder which shades off into a question, one of the fundamental metaphysical questions, a question which reinstates all the problems. If nothing "explains" or "resembles" this unspeakable stress of pitch, if I "taste self but at one tankard, that of my own being," "from what then do I with all my being and above all that taste of self, that selfbeing, come?" [7]

3

The proof of the existence of God for Hopkins is neither from the evidence of the external world, nor from direct intuition. It is a logical deduction from the fact of one's own uniqueness:

Nothing finite then can either begin to exist or eternally have existed of itself, because nothing can in the order of time or even of nature act before it exists or exercise function and determination before it has a nature to "function" and determine, to selve and instress, with. 8

And if this is true for all created things, how much more true for human beings is it that they cannot be self-created and self-existent. In a radical about-face Hopkins sees that his apparently so independent self must, on the evidence of its very nature, depend on something outside of itself, must draw its existence from "one of finer or higher pitch and determination than itself." 9 So here, almost in the moment of rejoicing over the distinctiveness of the "taste of oneself," strikes the "terror" of God. 10 For if the Creator could do so much, so can he undo, or do with his creatures as he wishes. For Hopkins, "a self is an absolute which stands to the absolute of God as the infinitesimal to the infinite." 11 The question becomes, then, "What relation do I or should I have to this Being who is so infinitely my superior and so 'dangerous' 12 to me?"

The answer is simple and total: "Man was created. Like the rest then to praise, reverence, and serve God; to give him glory." 13 But how do God's creatures "give him glory"? Merely by being themselves, by doing themselves. Selfhood is not a static possession, but an activity:

> Each mortal thing does one thing and the same:
> Deals out that being indoors each one dwells;
> Selves-goes itself; myself it speaks and spells;
> Crying What I do is me: for that I came. 14

But it is just here that a radical division among God's

creatures appears. Each non-human creature exists in the absolute security of being unable to do other than what it came for. It cannot choose not "to fling out broad its name," [15] and, in doing so, "make [God] known," "tell of him," "give him glory." [16] What they can *they always* do." [17] But if man can mean to give God glory, he can, necessarily, mean not to give him glory. His complete fulfillment of his nature, the selving for which he came, is radically contingent. If the full accomplishment of his being puts him "beyond all visible creatures," [18] so also he can, because of his free will and its accompanying self-consciousness utterly fail to be, in a way no other of God's creatures can. So then, within the very development of Hopkins' apprehension of the nature of his self-being an amazing transformation takes place. What had seemed so solid and definite turns out to be merely a "positive infinitesimal," [19] something that both exists and does not exist, like a point on a line. It is the mere potentiality of being, a self "intrinsically different from every other self," but a self to which a "nature" must be added. [20] What had seemed so self-subsistent is really very much like the Mallarméan "néant"; it is "nothing, a zero, in the score or account of existence": [21] "For the self before nature is no thing as yet but only possible; with the accession of a nature it becomes properly a self, for instance a person." [22]

Now we can see how the fearful experience recorded in the "terrible sonnets," utter paralysis of the will, and the accompanying spiritual vertigo, is possible, perhaps even necessary, given the premises of Hopkins' universe. Only the self-conscious mind of man can utterly fail to be and plunge downward into the abyss of complete nothingness, and only the mind of man can experience the terror of that plunge:

> O the mind, mind has mountains; cliffs of fall
> Frightful, sheer, no-man-fathomed. Hold them cheap
> May who ne'er hung there. Nor does long our small
> Durance deal with that steep or deep. [23]

And if it is only man who can taste himself, can be aware of his own being, it is also only man for whom that self-taste can be a terrifying experience of his isolation from God and from all things, an experience of complete enclosure within the prison of his own self-tormenting self:

> I am gall, I am heartburn. God's most deep decree
> Bitter would have me taste: my taste was me. [24]

The self which had seemed so solid, so enduring and self-subsistent discovers not only that it is created, but that it absolutely required help from outside itself in order to be, since to be necessarily means being able to selve, to do one's proper being. Without some relation to something outside oneself, man may remain paralyzed, a mere "positive infinitesimal," unable to transform possibility into actuality. Exiled within itself, caged in itself, the self discovers that far from sufficing to itself, it is, in its isolation, entirely impotent, as impotent as a eunuch. It is "time's eunuch," [25] that is, it is wholly unable to project into the future an action and then carry that action out. Instead of a growth, change, accomplishment matching the passage of time and filling it, such as we find in non-human creatures, man in his desolation finds that he is plunged into a subterranean darkness where time has lengthened out into an endless succession of empty moments, each one of which, because of its emptiness, seems itself to be lifelong:

> What hours, O what black hours we have spent
> This night! what sights you, heart, saw; ways you went!
> And more must, in yet longer light's delay.
>   With witness I speak this. But where I say
> Hours I mean years, mean life. [26]

In this extremity, any possibility of help will be grasped. Perhaps that non-human world of creatures who "always do what they can," even though it rebuffs man with "blank unlikeness," may serve in some way to rescue man from

6

his dizzy plunge into the abyss, from the utter cessation of the forward movement of his life. What is the relation of man to nature in Hopkins?

There is evident in Hopkins, from the earliest fragmentary notebooks onward, an interest in the exact nature of things in the external world which is extraordinary even in a century to which nature meant so much.

Hopkins' primary relation to nature was what perhaps remains man's most profound reaction to the external world: it was simply the astonished recognition that each perceived object is there, exists as a stubborn, irreducible fact. "But indeed," says Hopkins, "I have often felt . . . that nothing is so pregnant and straightforward to the truth as simple yes and is." [27] No one has felt more deeply and consciously this wonder at the mere existence of things, and no one has tried more earnestly to cherish that wonder and make it persist throughout as the basic ingredient of his relation to the world.

This attitude toward nature reminds one, of course, of the fidelity to the minute particulars of nature in Hopkins' contemporaries, the Pre-Raphaelites. Hopkins' own beautiful landscape drawings are very Pre-Raphaelite in their ornate realism. Often a sketch will accompany a detailed verbal description in the *Journal*. And the *Journal* itself is largely made up of the impersonal recording of observed phenomena:

Clouds however solid they may look far off are I think wholly made of film in the sheet or in the tuft. The bright woolpacks that pelt before a gale in a clear sky are in the tuft and you can see the wind unravelling and rending them finer than any sponge till within one easy reach overhead they are morselled to nothing and consumed—it depends of course on their size. [28]

There is in this a naturalism, an empiricism, even a nominalism, which seems to exclude any theory that objects in nature are parts of a coherent whole. What is, is what it is, and there seems to be nothing more to say about it. In any individual act of perception the whole world is reduced to the self and the observed scene, and one can only assert truthfully what one has oneself experienced. There is an implicit rejection of authority, of *a priori* ideas, the same rejection that was behind the growth of modern science, the same rejection that is one of the central motivations of romanticism. The Hopkins who wrote such passages in his journal might have said, with Keats, "O for a Life of Sensations rather than of Thoughts," and "I can never feel certain of any truth but from a clear perception of its Beauty." In order to reach truth one must begin all over again each time, reject all received opinions and make oneself energetically passive.

But what does Hopkins find outside of himself through this process of long and hard looking? He discovers that each thing is uniquely itself, that each thing has its own distinct nature, a nature which is never repeated. This individuality is manifested in things by the freshness and sharpness of their outline or pattern. Hopkins' nature is a nature with clearly defined edges. It is a nature without blurring or smudging, a nature in which each thing stands out vividly as though it were surrounded by perfectly translucid air. And air can reach all the surfaces of even the smallest and most intricate object, so abrupt is the frontier between the object and its surroundings:

> Wild air, world-mothering air,
> Nestling me everywhere,
> That each eyelid or hair
> Girdles; goes home betwixt
> The fleeciest, frailest-flixed
> Snowflake. [29]

Hopkins' word for the design or pattern which is the perceptible sign of the unique individuality of a thing is "inscape." I give only one example among a great many: "Below at a little timber bridge I looked at some delicate fly shafted ashes—there was one especially of single sonnet-like inscape." [30] But an "inscape" need not be a single object. It can be a *group* of objects which together form a pattern. Nevertheless, this form of inscape, too, is not a mere extrinsic organization of disparate parts, but is the manifestation of an inner, organic unity. Nor is inscape only discovered through the sense of sight (although that sense certainly predominates in Hopkins). The use of synesthesia in Hopkins' poetry is matched by an explicit analysis in the *Journal* of the way the unitary inscape of a single object may be perceived by all the senses. The passage begins: "The bluebells in your hand baffle you with their inscape, made to every sense." [31] "Inscape," then, is always used in contexts wherein the oneness, the organic unity, of a single object or group of *composed* objects is seen. And it is always associated with distinctness of outline, with words like "sharp," "wiry" and "crisp." Each object in Hopkins' world is distinctly itself, separated starkly from every other object in the universe. And it is not, like the nature of Tennyson and Rilke, seen as suspended statically and mutely in an eternal and fateful present which seems to be in the very act of fading suddenly away into non-existence. Nature in Hopkins is neither static nor does it hauntingly slip beyond the observer's immediate grasp. It is seen as present to the observer and as acting directly upon him without any intervening distance or vacancy. It does not somehow escape the spectator by withdrawing in upon itself. And even a natural scene which might seem to ask to be treated as static and inanimate is perceived by Hopkins as the center of a vital activity, even of a *personal* activity: "The mountain ranges, as any series or body of inanimate like things not often seen, have the air of persons and of interrupted activity." [32]

Natural objects, then, are not dead, but are sustained from within by a vital pressure. They are not static but ceaselessly active, even when they are apparently motionless. It is this inner pressure, permeating all nature, which

9

is the true source of inscape and what is actually manifested by it. The word is *in*-scape, the outer manifestation or "scape" of an inner principle or activity—not the mere external pattern which things make and which is pleasing to the eye as design: *"All the world is full of inscape* and chance left free to act falls into an order as well as purpose: looking out of my window I caught it in the random clods and broken heaps of snow made by the cast of a broom." [33] "There lives the dearest freshness deep down things." [34] "Fineness, proportion of feature, comes from a moulding force which succeeds in asserting itself over the resistance of cumbersome or restraining matter." [35] Some of Hopkins' drawings are startlingly like Chinese paintings: their swirling whirlpool patterns seem to manifest an ubiquitous spiritual force rolling through all nature. Hopkins' nature, as much as Coleridge's or Whitehead's, is the locus of a vital process, the explosive meeting-point of a spiritual elan and the stubborn resistance of matter. It is a nature which is in ceaseless activity and which manifests an extreme tension between the inner energy and the restraining outward form. The inscape is the meeting place of these two.

But for the inner energy itself Hopkins uses another word, a word which suggests not the outer design or pattern of a thing, but that very energy which upholds it from within: "all things are upheld by instress and are meaningless without it," wrote Hopkins in an undergraduate essay on Parmenides. [36] Just as the apparently unique and solid "taste of self" which was discovered in the first moment of awareness turned out to be a mere "positive infinitesimal," so nature, apparently so full of sharply defined distinctive objects, turns out to be upheld by a single permeating spirit. This spirit is God himself: "As we drove home the stars came out thick: I leant back to look at them and my heart opening more than usual praised our Lord to and in whom all that beauty comes home." [37] Even more striking is a passage from Hopkins' unpublished retreat notes of 1882. In this passage all the solid world is dissolved into expression of God. It is a passage which seems at the furthest possible remove from the naturalism, the humble scientific observation of nature with which Hopkins began: "God's utterance of Himself in Himself is God the Word, outside Himself in this world. The world then is word, expression, news of God. Therefore its end, its purpose, its purport, its meaning and its life and work is to name and praise him." [38] Nature, then, for Hopkins as for the Middle Ages, is the "book of nature" in which we may read "news of God." But there is one crucial difference: the medieval doctrine of analogy has almost disappeared from Hopkins. For the Christian of the middle ages each object in the natural world repeated some particular aspect of the supernatural world. It was thus a means of knowing that supernatural world in detail. For Hopkins all the world is "charged with the grandeur of God," and we know through the things of this world simply the power and presence of God, not details of the supernatural world.

It is easy to see now why Hopkins was so elated when in 1872 he discovered Duns Scotus' *Commentaries on the Sentences of Peter Lombard*, and why in that year he could write: "just then when I took in any inscape of the sky or sea I thought of Scotus." [39] Hopkins found in Scotus confirmation of the theory of nature and of the human self which he already held. Hopkins had always felt that the unique individuality of a thing or person was really a part of it, part of its form and not merely a result of the matter in which the form was actualized as Aristotle and St. Thomas maintained. He had always felt that one knows in the act of perception not, by means of the Aristotelean or Thomistic *"species intelligibilis,"* the mere *"quidditas"* or "whatness" of a thing, but its distinctive individuality, its "thisness." In the Scotian doctrine of the *haecceitas* or individualizing form, which makes an object not simply a member of a species, a pine tree, for example, but this particular unrepeatable pine tree, Hopkins found his own deepest apprehension of the world systematized. And perhaps even more importantly Hopkins felt that through the immediate sense perception of things in the world he could know God directly as the "instress" that upheld each thing. He did not want a world of abstract "ideas" or "forms" ("pinetreeness," "bluebellness" and so on) to intervene between himself and God. Paradoxically, the Scotian metaphysic which, from one perspective at least, seems perilously close to nominalism, [40] was actually a much better basis for Hopkins' view of the universe as "news of God" than would have been the Aristotelean theory of forms. Only a world in which God himself is directly present without intermediary in each one of his creatures can be "expression, news of God" in the way Hopkins deeply felt it to be: "All things," he wrote, "therefore are charged with love, are charged with God and if we know how to touch them give off sparks and take fire, yield drops and flow, ring and tell of him." [41]

IV

"If we know how to touch them." The perception of the instress in natural objects, then, is contingent on something in the observer. The true theme of Hopkins' *Journal* and of his nature poems is not nature alone but the man-nature relationship. Hopkins has a striking phrase for the "bridge," the dynamic interaction, he felt to exist between subject and object: he called it the "stem of stress between us and things." [42] This tension, as between two magnets, is absolutely necessary to "bear us out and carry the mind over." [43] Subject and object share one thing at least in common: their possession of the inward energy of instress. This intrinsic spiritual force flashes out from objects; it rays forth from them. Each object is not merely the tense withholding of a spiritual charge. This charge leaps out at the slightest provocation, and all objects are thereby potentially in touch with one another. The world in Hopkins is a vast network of electrical discharges given and received by objects which are an inexhaustible source of the divine energy:

> The world is charged with the grandeur of God.
> It will flame out, like shining from shook foil. [44]

But human beings too are charged with energy: "Honour is flashed off exploit," says Hopkins, [45] and "self flashes off frame and face." [46] Perception, as in Whitehead, is only a special case of the dynamic interaction between all objects. In the moment of perception a "stem of stress" is created between subject and object to which the subject contributes as much as does the object: "What you look hard at seems to look hard at you." [47] Hopkins' epistemology, like that of the Pre-Socratics (whom he had read), is based ultimately on the "theory of sensation by like and like." [48] Only if the beholder is able to return stress for stress will the moment of knowledge, the moment of the coalescence of subject and object, take place.

Hopkins almost always mentions both subject and object in his descriptions of nature. He not only describes the bluebells, he says: "I caught as well as I could while my companions talked the Greek rightness of their beauty." [49] "I caught." It is an active verb, suggesting the energetic grasp of the mind on things. The phrase echoes through the *Journal* and the poetry; it is Hopkins' special term for the strenuous activity of perception: "I caught this morning morning's minion, kingdom of daylight's dauphin, dapple-dawn-drawn Falcon." [50]

Just as Hopkins' self-awareness is an organic taste of himself, not a dry lucidity, so his grasp of the external world in the dynamic moment of instress is as much emotional as intellectual. It is a total possession of the object by the thinking, feeling, sensing subject. The object is internalized by the subject. Hence Hopkins speaks repeatedly of instress as something deeply *felt*, not merely intellectually realized: "But such a lovely damasking in the sky as today I never felt before." [51] "Looking all round but most in looking far up the valley I felt an instress and charm of Wales." [52] One gathers from the constant use of this word and of the word "caught" a strong sense of the precariousness of these experiences. They are reported with a tone of elation, as though they were rare occurrences of success among many failures.

And sometimes indeed the instress does fail to come. It depends on just the proper conditions in the perceiver and in what is perceived: in the perceiver a certain freshness of vision and a singleness of concentration on the object perceived: "Unless you refresh the mind from time to time you cannot always remember or believe how deep the inscape in things is." [53] For the instress to come it must be as if there were nothing else in the world but the present moment of ecstatic communication with what is directly present to the senses. Hopkins differs from the romantic poets generally in that there is in his writings almost no interest in affective memory, in the linkage to a moment in the past by means of intense perception in the present. Each moment recorded in the *Journal* and in the poems is sufficient unto itself. There is a kind of radical discontinuity in Hopkins' temporal existence. It proceeds by a series of vivid perceptions. Each is distinct from all the others and each fades away almost immediately to be replaced by another or sometimes by mere vacancy and lassitude. If a relation between past and present *via* memory appears in Hopkins at all it is almost always in the form of a lament for the irretrievable fading away of the ecstacy of instress when it is past: "Saw a lad burning big bundles of dry honey-suckle: the flame (though it is no longer freshly in my mind) was brown and gold." [54] The *Journal* entries were often written down long after the event recorded from notes made at the time. In the few cases where the notes themselves exist we can sense a frantic attempt to capture some portion at least of what is known to be fleeting and fragile. And are not the *Journal* and the poems themselves ultimately to be defined as the attempt to give through words some form of permanence to what were actually unique, instantaneous and unrepeatable experiences? There is implicit in the very form of the *Journal* and of the poems a deep anguish at the inevitable passing away of these moments. The loss of these experiences is painful because it is the loss of what the person himself is at that moment. We can detect in the *Journal* both the anxious attempt to give these fleeting moments some permanence in words and the obsessive urge to have more and more and more of them. Hopkins can think of no more painful form of self-mortification and penance than to deprive himself of the repetition of one of these experiences. [55]

But sometimes even if the precious activity of instressing is permitted and desired it will not come. Not only must one banish the past and future and live wholly in the moment, one must also banish the awareness that any other person exists: "Even with one companion ecstacy is almost banished: you want to be alone and to feel that, and leisure—all pressure taken off." [56] One can see clearly and explicitly here what is sometimes obscured in other projects of founding one's self-identity on a direct relationship to nature: such a project is, strictly speaking, amoral. It does not exist in what Kierkegaard called the "ethical" realm. For Hopkins, as for Keats and Wordsworth, the self is formed not through inter-personal relations but through experiences of non-human nature, experiences which simply ignore the existence of other human beings. Hopkins' *Journal* and his greatest poems are the record of experiences of absolute isolation from other people.

But even to be alone, in the moment, isolated from past and future and from all other human beings is not always enough. There may be simply a failure of the sensibility, a failure which in some people is total and permanent: "I thought how sadly beauty of inscape was unknown and buried away from simple people and yet how near at hand it was if they had eyes to see it and it could be called out everywhere again." [57]

And sometimes it is the object which for one reason or another fails to offer itself to perception, fails to flash itself outwards in the stress that can be counterstressed by the poet. This fact is perceived when a change in a natural

15

object makes it possible to detect an inscape that has been present all the time, but hidden: "This is the time to study inscape in the spraying of trees, for the swelling buds carry them to a pitch which the eye could not else gather." [58] "I caught as well as I could [in the bluebells] . . . a notable glare the eye may abstract and sever from the blue color of light beating up from so many glassy heads, which like water is good to float their deeper instress in upon the mind." [59] "Float their deeper instress in upon the mind"! How different this is from the perception, at a distance, that each individual thing is its distinct self and has an inscape. How Hopkins wants to possess that external perception, to internalize it, to "float it in upon the mind" across the stem of stress between subject and object.

When the communication is total perceiver and perceived come into intimate contact, interpenetrate and coalesce. This experience is the true theme of the early nature poems, of "Spring," "The Starlit Night," "The Sea and the Skylark," and "Hurrahing in Harvest." The effect of this experience on the self is, in the etymological sense of the word, "ecstacy": the self leaps outside of itself and creates a new self by means of a substantial identification with all of perceived nature:

> These things, these things were here and but the beholder
> > Wanting; which two when they once meet,
> The heart rears wings bold and bolder
> > And hurls for him, O half hurls earth for him off under
> > > his feet. [60]

V

Another night from the gallery window I saw a brindled heaven, the moon just marked—I *read* a broad careless inscape flowing throughout. [61]

The [elms'] tops are touched and *worded* with leaf. [62]
On the one hand, natural objects are intelligible; they

16

can be read by man as though they were not simply objects, but *signs*. On the other hand, they are *mute* signs. They only speak when there is a human being present to read them. Man gives natural objects a voice and a language. In "reading" them, and in bodying forth that meaning in words man gives nature something it does not possess, self-consciousness and a tongue to speak that awareness:

> And what is Earth's eye, tongue, or heart else, where
> Else, but in dear and dogged man? [63]

The true "stem of stress" between man and nature is the word itself. At the point of fusion, where subject meets object and coalesces with it, is born the word. Words have for Hopkins a magic quality of attaining the object, wresting from it its meaning and making that meaning a permanent possession for man. "To every word meaning a thing and not a relation," wrote Hopkins in a brief paper on words dated 1868, "belongs a passion or prepossession or enthusiasm which it has the power of suggesting or producing, but not always or in everyone." [64] In one sense, all Hopkins' efforts in his poetry were towards the creation of a continuum of words which would, like a proper name, convey the "prepossession," to use his word, of a unique individual experience. All Hopkins' poetry is based on the fundamental discovery that words can imitate things, re-present them in a different form, rescue them from the ceaselessly moving realm of nature and translate them into the permanent realm of words. Words can, Hopkins' discovered, "catch" things, "stall" them, as he said, [65] and transform them into spiritual stuff. Metaphors were not, for him, "poetic lies," nor were words arbitrary signs. Hopkins discovered what certain contemporary poets, philosophers and anthropologists are making their central theme: in the word subject and object merge and we touch the object in a way we never can without naming it. The word is not an arbitrary label; it carries the object alive into the heart. Each different word for the

17

"same thing" transmits to the mind a slightly (or radically) different aspect of reality. Each new word is a window through which a new portion of reality is revealed. To name a thing is to perceive it. This thing is not subjective, not "imposed" by the mind "outwards." [66] It is "really there," but is only perceived when it is so named. We only truly *see* the world when we have represented it in words. Metaphor, onomatopoeia, compound words, inversion, functional shift, and all the other special techniques of verbal representation are only modes of the universal operation of verbal *mimesis*. All the seemingly idiosyncratic methods of Hopkins' poetry are, in one way, directed towards the perfect imitation in words of the object perceived in all its concreteness and in all its energetic activity.

But if words for Hopkins face outwards towards the object, they also face inwards towards the mind. Even in the earliest of Hopkins' writings we can see another fundamental obsession: a fascination for words in themselves, for their etymology, for their multiplicity of meanings, for their abstract "pre-possession" without any reference to particular experiences. Hopkins was very sensitive to the inscape of words in themselves, taken in isolation from their meaning. He was fascinated by the fact that the same word can in different contexts carry the "prepossession" of entirely different realities: "Sky peak'd with tiny flames. . . . Altogether peak is a good word. For sunlight through shutter, locks of hair, rays in brass knobs, etc. Meadows peaked with flowers." [67] If Hopkins was the most nature-intoxicated poet of the Victorian period, he was also the poet most fascinated by words in themselves, by words not as the signs of an external reality but as the signs of certain definite spiritual states.

Accordingly, alongside the theory and practice of poetry as *mimesis* we can observe a very different notion, a notion of poetry as a thing to be contemplated for its own sake and without any reference to the external world: "But as air, melody, is what strikes me most of all in music and design in painting, so design, pattern or what I am in the habit of calling 'inscape' is what I above all aim at in poetry." [68] Inscape, said Hopkins, is "the very soul of art." [69] It is what makes a work of art "beautiful to individuation," that is, it gives a poem or a painting the kind of distinctness, uniqueness, *haecceitas*, possessed by a natural object. "Inscape," then, has two very different meanings. It can refer to the willed design of a human artifact as well as to the pattern into which objects fall without any human intervention.

Hopkins sought to achieve in his poetry an organic unity in which each part would be interrelated to all the other parts, and thus transcend its isolation as the name of an external object: "Repetition, *oftening, over-and-overing, aftering* of the inscape must take place in order to detach it to the mind and in this light poetry is speech which alters and often its inscape, speech couched in a repeated figure and verse as spoken sound having a repeated figure." [70] "Tout le mystère est la," said Mallarmé, in terms that Hopkins himself might have used, "établir les identités secrètes par un deux à deux qui ronge et use les objêts, au nom d'une centrale pureté." [71] For Hopkins, as for Mallarmé, the repetition or parallelism which establishes "secret identities" between one part of a poem and another was for the sake of a "central purity," a central purity which Hopkins called the total inscape of the poem. Here we have moved very far indeed from the notion of poetry as the *mimesis* of the external world, as the violent point of contact between subject and object. All the density of texture in Hopkins' verse is as much for the sake of creating its own self-sufficient durée or "sliding inscape," as it is to express the packed energy and radiance which some event in nature contains. If the extreme use of various forms of "over-and-overing" in Hopkins, assonance, alliteration, internal rhyme, Welsh *cynghanedd* and so on, is in one sense all for the purpose of representing nature, it is in another sense wholly indifferent to external nature and all calculated to "detach the

19

mind" and "carry" the "inscape of speech for the inscape's sake."

Inscape in poetry is "the essential and only lasting thing";[72] it is "species or individually distinctive beauty of style." [73] But it is only attained *via* the individuality of the poet himself: "Every poet," says Hopkins, "must be original and originality a condition of poetic genius; so that each poet is like a species in nature (*not* an *individuum genericum* or *specificum*) and can never recur." [74] Each poet, then, is very like each inanimate object in that he is a *species*, not a *genus*, a *haecceitas*, not a *quidditas*. "No doubt my poetry errs on the side of oddness," wrote Hopkins, ". . . Now it is the virtue of design, pattern, or inscape to be distinctive and it is the vice of distinctiveness to become queer. This vice I cannot have escaped." [75] We can see now that when Hopkins said that he aimed above all at "inscape" in poetry he meant not simply that he aimed at pattern, design, organic unity, but that he aimed at these because only through them could poetry be the affirmation and actualization of his own identity. So in the headnote of the sonnet to Henry Purcell, Purcell is praised for having "uttered in notes the very make and species of man as created in him and in all men generally." [76] But in the poem itself the bow to St. Thomas is forgotten and Purcell's music is praised not as manifesting "man generally," but as the expression of an absolutely unique self, Purcell's own "arch-especial . . . spirit":

It is the forgèd feature finds me; it is the rehearsal
Of own, of abrúpt sélf there so thrusts on, so throngs
    the ear. [77]

But at the center of the project of individuation by means of "poeting" there lies a double flaw, a flaw which leads to the faltering and ultimate total collapse of the project. In this collapse, Hopkins is left bare again, "no one, nowhere," enclosed within the unpierced walls of his own impotent taste of self.

VI

This collapse can be seen from two perspectives. The poet, it is true, however much he may be apparently imitating the external world in his poetry, is actually speaking himself, *doing* himself. The poet poets. But this "poeting" is accomplished after all through words that have meanings, that remain signs even when they are used for the sake of their own inscapes. A poem is not an act of absolute self-creation. Without the external world it could not exist; however independent it may be it must remain, to be successful, a faithful representation of the external world. The success of this reliance on the external world will depend on the stability and solidity of that world itself.

Hopkins' nature, so densely packed with distinctly singular objects, each sustained by the instress of an inexhaustible energy would seem perfectly suited to such a dependence on it. Nevertheless, we can see a disastrous transition in Hopkins' apprehension of nature. At first it seems full of solid, static, enduring objects, objects which cannot help but be themselves and which cannot cease to be themselves. But it becomes apparent that these things are in continual movement. Nature is not only full of kinetic energy, it is also a nature in process which is the dynamic expending of that energy. One remembers the clouds in "Hurrahing in Harvest" which are continually made and unmade, "moulded ever and melted across skies." [78] It is only in some kind of movement that things can radiate their inexhaustible energy outwards. But there seems nothing ominous about the discovery that things are not fixed eternally in a single inscape.

Yet in two magnificent poems of Hopkins' maturity, "Spelt from Sibyl's Leaves" and "That Nature is a Heraclitean Fire and of the Comfort of the Resurrection," there is a complete reversal of the earlier feeling of the permanent distinctiveness of things. What had begun as the simple perception that the inscapes of things are in a continual process of change becomes an anguished recognition that the "forgéd features" of things are ultimately utterly destroyed. Never has the perception of nature as a shifting flux of birth and death been expressed with more intensity. As in Parmenides, "unmeaning (*aoan*) night, thick and wedgèd body" [79] which inevitably follows day and hides the perceptible forms of things is taken as the symbol of that absolute non-being which will inevitably overtake all created things, all *mortal* beauty:

Earnest, earthless, equal, attuneable, ' vaulty, voluminous, . . . stupendous
Evening strains to be time's vást ' womb-of-all, home-of-all, hearse-of-all night.

   . . . For earth ' her being has unbound, her dapple is at an end, as —
tray or aswarm, all throughther, in throngs; ' self in self steepèd and páshed — qúite
Disremembering, dismémbering ' áll now. [80]

Only if we know how much Hopkins cherished the "original definiteness and piquant beauty of things" [81] can we understand fully what violence of regret, what "pity and indignation," [82] there is in the image of "self in self steeped and pashed." It is a dynamically *experienced* image of the return of all individuated forms to the "thick and wedged body" of primordial chaos. In that chaos every self will be blurred, smeared, inextricably mixed in the other selves. Nature will be, in Hopkins' striking coinage, "all throughther." The suggestion that a complete phrase such as "each interpenetrated through and through with the others" has been collapsed into "throughther" makes it a perfect *mimesis* of the event described. One feels the forms of the collapsed words straining to differentiate themselves, just as the identities being crushed into chaos resist desperately the unbinding of their being.

In the poem called "That Nature is a Heraclitean Fire" another of the Pre-Socratic symbols is used, fire, the symbol of the energy of being, "ethery flame of fire" as Hopkins calls it in his essay on Parmenides. [83] In this poem all the thousand forms in which this energy manifests itself are seen to be impermanent as clouds or as straws in a bonfire, and are continually being destroyed and replaced by other forms. "God gave things," wrote Hopkins, "a forward and perpetual motion." [84] If "Spelt from Sibyl's Leaves" is the frightening vision of night as dismembering, the later poem is a hymn to day as destructive fire, a fire in which "million-fuèled, nature's bonfire burns on." [85] The very energy of Being, its fire, what seemed to inhere within things and to sustain them in selfhood turns out to be itself the source of their undoing. For that energy drives things on to an activity of selving that eventually consumes them, unselves them, transforms them out of all resemblance to their former selves. Only the "ethery flame of fire" remains constant, that and the activity of change itself, the ceaseless metamorphosis of one form into another.

How, then, can an identification of oneself with external nature be used to establish a permanent identity if nature is as unstable as the day which moves every moment closer towards the tomb of night, as quick to change and as destructive as fire and if it is to this universal flux that we must testify in our poems?

VII

The evidence from the other side is equally fatal. If nature fails man, man fails nature and fails himself even more totally. His relation to nature can be far different from the reverent and concentrated attention which "floats its instress in upon the mind." If natural objects lack stability and permanence, so even more completely does man. In non-human nature the law is transformation, flux, but the law for man is absolute destruction, since his identity, though incarnated, is too subtle, too spiritual, to retain its distinctness through even so many changes as a tree or flower will endure. The final lesson man learns

23

from nature is that he, too, is part of nature and that this means but one thing for him: death. If all objects are burned in nature's bonfire, man is simply annihilated in that same fire:

> But quench her bonniest, dearest ' to her, her clearest-
> selvèd spark
> Man, how fast his firedint, ' his mark on mind, is gone!
> Both are in an unfathomable, all is in an enormous dark
> Drowned. [86]

Even if a man could achieve through the poetizing of his perception of nature an unwavering and permanent identity, it would be all dismembered and unbound in a moment at his death.

But even within the limits of earthly life the project is bound to fail. As we have seen, the ability to "instress" nature is intermittent and can be replaced in a moment by the most agonizing spiritual impotence. If the self is unable to selve, as it often is, it will be cut off entirely from the world which can give it such delight. In times of spiritual dryness, of spiritual paralysis, the self is locked entirely within its self-torment and cut off entirely from the outside world:

> I cast for comfort I can no more get
> By groping round my comfortless, than blind
> Eyes in their dark can day or thirst can find
> Thirst's all-in-all in a world of wet. [87]

The proper image of spiritual aridity is not of a thirsty man in a desert but of a thirsty man in the midst of water he cannot drink; it is not the image of a man straining to see in the darkness but of a blind man in the midst of light which he cannot see.

There was something ominous in the double orientation of words, and in the split in Hopkins between poetry as *mimesis* and poetry as "the inscape of speech for the inscape's sake." Words can become not the point of fusion of subject and object, but the locus of their most absolute

24

and permanent division. Words, instead of reaching out to things, touching them, and *giving* them over to man, can become merely the opaque walls of his interior prison:

> . . . Only what word
> Wisest my heart breeds dark heaven's baffling ban
> Bars or hell's spell thwarts. This to hoard unheard
> Heard unheeded, leaves me a lonely began. [88]

Cast outwards by the mind to capture the object, words may fall endlessly through a shadowy void and never touch anything at all, neither things nor the God within things:

> . . . my lament
> Is cries countless. cries like dead letters sent
> To dearest him that lives alas! away. [89]

The end point of Hopkins' long dialogue with nature is a complete reversal of the ecstatic mood of "Hurrahing in Harvest." He is cut off entirely from nature and lives in the utter isolation of his spiritual inertia, "this tormented mind / With this tormented mind tormenting yet." [90] His state is very like that of the damned who are also imprisoned in the corrosive contemplation of their own limits. "Against these acts of its own," wrote Hopkins, "the lost spirit dashes itself like a caged beast and is in prison, violently instresses them and burns, stares into them and is the deepest darkened." [91]

VIII

If all the positive ways of self-affirmation fail, perhaps there is one final way, a way through the center of the deepest despair and spiritual abnegation: the creation of one's true self by self-sacrifice. The crucifixion, central moment of history, was the act whereby Christ "annihilated himself." [92] Christ was most Christ, the Mediator and Saviour of mankind, when he thus sacrificed himself, just as the windhover is most windhover when it renounces its sovereignty of the air and dives earthward.

Hopkins in his later years planned a treatise on sacrifice. It was never published, but it is clear from texts scattered throughout his work what he would have said. Nonhuman things can praise God simply by being themselves, by "dealing out that being indoors each one dwells." Only man in order to praise God and win salvation must cease to be himself. Only through such a total change of his essential being can man escape the damnation of being "no one, nowhere, / In wide the world's weal," exiled within himself, separated from all, dwelling in "the barren wilderness outside of God," [93] condemned to taste his own self eternally. Only by ceasing to be oneself and becoming Christ can a man avoid an existence which is a continual dizzy falling away in time:

> I am a soft sift
> In an hourglass-at the wall
> Fast, but mined with a motion, a drift,
> And it crowds and it combs to the fall. [94]

In the subtle and elaborate investigation of free will and grace in the "Commentary on the Spiritual Exercises of St. Ignatius Loyola" Hopkins devises a brilliant metaphor to define this transformation. The actual pitch of self existing at any moment in each person is only one self out of an infinity of possible selves. It is like one cross-section out of all the possible ones of a three-dimensional solid. It is one "cleave of being" out of the total "burl of being." This "burl of being" is as much really part of a person, though only potential, as his actual self. The transformation of the self when it becomes Christ is the abandonment of one cleave of being and the actualizing of another potential one. For every man, and even Satan himself, has at least one potential cross-section which coincides with Christ.

But how can this transformation be brought about? For man of his own power can do absolutely nothing to move himself from one "cleave of being" to another. There is only one answer: by God's grace, "which lifts the receiver from one cleave of being to another and to a vital act in Christ." [95] Hopkins' concept of grace seems to relate him rather to Post-Reformation theologies than to Thomistic Catholicism. For a Thomist, the initial act of creation gives a man's soul an indestructible permanence. He cannot cease to be himself, even if he veers to one of the extremes of mortal sin or sainthood. Grace, in the Thomistic view, does not exert its power on the permanent identity of a man's being, but only upon the variations of his temporal existence. But grace for Hopkins is precisely a *transubstantiation* of the person's innermost being. It is "an exchange of one whole for another whole, as they say in the mystery of Transubstantiation, a conversion of the whole substance into another substance, but here it is not a question of substance; it is a lifting him from one self to another self, which is a most marvellous display of divine power." [96] "It is not a question of substance," says Hopkins, but it is difficult to say what else it is, this total transformation from one self to another self, "through the gulf and void between pitch and pitch of being." [97]

Where then is free will? It would seem that there is nothing left for God's creature to do but to pray for grace. But in what Hopkins calls the "least sigh of desire," the "aspiration," [98] of man towards God a tiny corner is left for man's free will. "Correspondence" is the key word in Hopkins' theory of grace. Just as man's salvation is won by achieving a correspondence to Christ, so the only action on man's part that makes this occur is the minute movement of volition whereby he wills to correspond with God's grace: "and by this infinitesimal act the creature does what in it lies to bridge the gulf fixed between its present actual and worser pitch of will and its future better one." [99] This "correspondence with grace and seconding of God's designs" [100] is man's tiny bit contributed towards the creation of his own best self.

But even when transubstantiated into Christ a man still remains himself, since it is that mere positive infinitesimal which the man is aware of in his first self-consciousness which is so filled with Christ. The proper figure for the achieved transformation is of a hollow shell or vessel which is everywhere inhabited by Christ and brought into positive being by Christ: "This too," writes Hopkins, "but brings out the nature of the man himself, as the lettering on a sail, or the device upon a flag are best seen when it fills." [101]

However, this metamorphosis of man into Christ remains until his death contingent, in jeopardy. It depends on God's continual gift to fresh grace and on man's continual "saying Yes" [102] to God. [103] Only at the Resurrection will man be securely and permanently transformed, soul and body, into Christ: whence the "comfort of the Resurrection," the only real comfort for man:

> . . . Flesh fade, and mortal trash
> Fall to the residuary worm, ' world's wildfire, leave but ash:
> In a flash, at a trumpet crash,
> I am all at once what Christ is, ' since he was what I am, and
> This Jack, joke, poor potsherd, ' patch, matchwood,
>   immortal diamond,
>   Is immortal diamond. [104]

We must leave Hopkins here, at the extreme point of his despair and hope, turned far from nature and from poetry, standing aghast at the sight of a world that is visibly disintegrating and being consumed, as at the last trump. We leave him with nothing but the "comfort of the resurrection," the hope of that miracle of transubstantiation which will change man from the mere impure carbon of matchwood to immortal diamond, change him, that is, from one allotropic form of himself to another so different that if there is any secret continuity between the two it is only in that the same null potentiality of being, is, in each case, actualized by God, actualized by God in ways that are as far apart as the whole distance from hell to heaven.

NOTES

1 Humphry House (ed..), *The Notebooks and Papers of Gerard Manley Hopkins* (London: Oxford University Press, 1937), p. 309.

2 *Ibid.*

3 *Ibid.*

4 *Ibid.,* p. 310.

5 *Ibid.*

6 W. H. Gardner (ed.), *Poems of Gerard Manley Hopkins,* Third Edition (New York: Oxford University Press, 1948), p. 73.

7 *Notebooks,* p. 310.

8 *Ibid.,* p. 312.

9 *Ibid.,* p. 309.

10 *Poems,* p. 56.

11 *Notebooks,* p. 331.

12 *Poems,* p. 73.

13 *Notebooks,* p. 303.

14 *Poems,* p. 95.

15 *Ibid.*

16 *Notebooks,* p. 303.

17 *Ibid.*

18 *Ibid.,* p. 303.

19 *Ibid..* p. 322.

20 *Ibid.*

21 *Ibid.*

22 *Ibid.,* p. 325.

23 *Poems,* p. 107.

24 *Ibid.,* p. 110.

25 *Ibid.,* p. 113.

26 *Ibid.,* p. 109.

27 *Notebooks,* p. 98.

28 *Ibid.,* p. 140.

29 *Poems,* p. 99.

30 *Notebooks,* p. 211.

31 *Ibid.,* p. 145.

32 W. H. Gardner (ed.), *Poems and Prose of Gerard Manley Hopkins* (London: Penguin Books, 1953), p. 115.

33 *Notebooks,* pp. 173, 174.

34 *Poems,* p. 70.

35 C. C. Abbott (ed.), *Further Letters of Gerard Manley Hopkins* (London: Oxford University Press, 1938), p. 159.

36 *Notebooks,* p. 98.

37 *Ibid.,* p. 205.

38 Quoted in W. A. M. Peters, S.J., *Gerard Manley Hopkins* (London: Oxford University Press, 1948), p. 175.

39 *Notebooks*, p. 161.

40 See Bernard Landry, *La Philosophie de Duns Scot* (Paris, 1922), *passim*.

41 *Notebooks*, p. 342.

42 *Ibid.*, p. 98.

43 *Ibid.*

44 *Poems*, p. 70.

45 *Ibid.*, p. 112.

46 *Ibid.*, p. 104.

47 *Notebooks*, p. 140.

48 *Ibid.*, p. 102.

49 *Ibid.*, p. 174.

50 *Poems*, p. 73.

51 *Notebooks*, p. 143.

52 *Ibid.*, p. 210.

53 *Ibid.*, p. 140.

54 *Ibid.*, p. 159.

55 See *Ibid.*, p. 199.

56 *Ibid.*, p. 111.

57 *Ibid.*, p. 161.

58 *Ibid.*, p. 141.

59 *Ibid.* p. 174.

60 *Poems*, p. 75.

61 *Notebooks* p. 158, my italics.

62 *Ibid.*, p. 190, my italics.

63 *Poems*, p. 96.

64 *Notebooks*, p. 95.

65 For a use of this word, see *Notebooks*, p. 127: "these images . . . once lodged there are stalled by the mind like other images."

66 *Ibid.*, p. 154.

67 *Ibid.*, p. 32.

68 C. C. Abbott (ed.), *Letters of Gerard Hopkins to Robert Bridges* (London: Oxford University Press, 1935), p. 60.

69 C. C. Abbott (ed.), *Correspondence of Gerard Manley Hopkins and Richard Watson Dixon* (London: Oxford University Press, 1935), p. 135.

70 *Notebooks*, p. 249.

71 Letter to Vielé Griffin, August 8, 1891, quoted in G. Poulet, *La Distance Intérieure* (Paris, 1952), p. 343.

72 *Further Letters*, p. 225.

73 *Ibid.*

74 *Ibid.*, p. 222.

75 *Letters to Bridges*, p. 60.

76 *Poems,* p. 84.
77 *Ibid.,* p. 85.
78 *Poems,* p. 74.
79 *Notebooks,* p. 102.
80 *Poems,* p. 104.
81 *Further Letters,* p. 72.
82 *Poems,* p. 112.
83 *Notebooks,* p. 102.
84 *Ibid.,* p. 347.
95 *Notebooks,* p. 337.
86 *Ibid.*
87 *Ibid.,* p. 111.
88 *Ibid.,* p. 109.
89 *Ibid.*
90 *Ibid.,* p. 110.
91 Peters, *op. cit.,* p. 177.
92 *Letters to Bridges,* p. 175.
93 *Notebooks,* p. 344.
94 *Poems,* p. 56.
95 *Notebooks,* p. 337.
96 *Ibid.,* p. 329.
97 *Ibid.,* pp. 334, 335.
98 *Ibid.,* p. 333.
99 *Ibid.*
100 *Ibid.,* p. 344.
101 *Ibid.,* p. 343.
102 *Ibid.,* p. 333.
103 See Hopkins' beautiful image for God's continual *sustaining* of man in stanza four of "The Wreck of the Deutschland" (*Poems,* p. 56).
104 *Poems,* p. 112.

Marjorie Downing

INSCAPE AND INSTRESS:
FURTHER ANALOGIES WITH SCOTUS

At the risk of setting up further waves of what Joyce calls the "true scholastic stink" I feel it necessary to add a few more observations to the many already made on the philosophic clarification of his own aesthetic position that Gerard Manley Hopkins found in Duns Scotus. The attention of critics is becoming more and more absorbed in studying the poetic process itself, the poet's perception of complexity and coherence, and his attempt to express them in terms of aesthetic structure. For such a study Hopkins offers rich materials. His own critical acumen forced him early to coin new terms, "inscape" and "instress," in order to express more accurately the nature of poetic insight and response. It is apparent, therefore, that the more we can find out about inscape and instress, the more fully we shall grasp the nature of Hopkins' poetic experience, and ultimately the quality of the poems to which it gave rise. It is this purpose which justifies further exploration into fourteenth-century philosophic subtleties.

The recent study of Hopkins by W. A. M. Peters [1] goes very nearly as far as a critic can go, it seems, in the analysis of the critical terms "inscape' and "instress" which are central to the poet's sensibility and technique. The early near-misses of writers like Elsie Elizabeth Phare, Francis MacManus, and Daniel Sargent have been supplanted by the collation and analysis of Hopkins' uses of the terms, and by the exploitation of the hints he gave us about the philosophic support he found in Duns Scotus. The various notebooks and papers, so rich and still so meager, will probably not yield much more for further definitions of inscape and instress than those Father Peters has proposed, but it is possible, I think, to clarify certain points by pursuing the analogies with Scotus even more closely than he and other critics have already done.

Hopkins' own statement that "design, pattern or what I am in the habit of calling 'inscape' is what I above all aim at in poetry. Now it is the virtue of design, pattern or inscape to be distinctive. . . ." (*Letters to Bridges,* p. 66), and his declaration that "All the world is full of inscape and chance left free to act falls into order as well as purpose," [2] have pointed the critics' way. Father Peters calls inscape "the unified complex of those sensible qualities of the object of perception that strikes us as inseparably belonging to and most typical of it, so that through the knowledge of this unified complex of sense-data we may gain an insight into the individual essence of the object" (p. 1). Here I have to quarrel with the emphasis on "sensible" and "sense-data," for reasons I shall explain later. But it is indeed this distinctive individuality of all objects of perception which is Hopkins' pivotal poetic concept.

The philosophic justification for inscape which Hopkins suggests that he discerned in Duns Scotus has helped to clarify our understanding of the term. In 1872 he read Scotus' commentaries on the *Sentences* of Peter Lombard and "was flush with a new stroke of enthusiasm." He wrote at that time, "It may come to nothing or it may be a mercy from God, but just then when I took in any inscape of the sky or sea I thought of Scotus" (*Notebooks,* p. 161).

The "mercy from God" lay undoubtedly in Scotus' analysis of the distinctive individuality, the inscape of objects of perception. For Scotus, "of reality the rarest-veined unraveller," individuation is not the result of matter quantitatively determined, as Thomas held, but of an *ultima realitas entis,* a last *formal* determination which restricts and completes in the individual the specific form. This ultimate determination, which Scotus calls the *haecceitas,* or this-ness, is neither matter alone nor form alone, *qua* matter and form, but is something that occurs equally to both, a positive objective modification which makes an object just exactly *this* object and no other (*Opus Oxonieuse,* II, d. iii, qu. 6, n. 15). The *haecceitas* is the individualizing difference restricting the specific form of a being and finally determining its essential individuality.

Hopkins was intensely conscious of the "abrupt self" which marks all things, and especially human nature, the "world within." While on a retreat in Liverpool in 1884, he speculated on the problem of identity, declaring:

I find myself both as man and as myself something most determined and distinctive, at pitch, more distinctive and higher pitched than anything else I see. . . . I consider my selfbeing, my consciousness and feeling of myself, that taste of myself, of *I* and *me* above and in all things, which is more distinctive than the taste of ale or alum, more distinctive than the smell of walnut leaf or camphor. . . . Nothing else in nature comes near this unspeakable stress of pitch, distinctiveness, and selving, this selfbeing of my own [*Notebooks,* p. 309].

Then, making the connection with Scotus explicit, he asked, "Is not this pitch or whatever we call it then the same as Scotus' *ecceitas?*" (*Notebooks,* p. 328).

"Whatever we call it" in metaphysics, inscape is what Hopkins called it in his patient, minute observations of the world of nature. He noted, for example, the individuality of Spanish chestnuts, "their inscape bold, jutty, somewhat oaklike" (*Notebooks,* p. 108). That inscape is not simply a metaphysical concept, a translation of *haecceitas,* but that it is rather a poetic approximation of a metaphysical reality is of course evident from Hopkins' attempts to express it in descriptive language. It is "to the eye" that inscape is restored to the "hangers and flying sprays of elms when you look at them from underneath and see every wave in every twig" (*Notebooks,* p. 130). Watching the graceful horned violet wither, he declared that "the flower ran through beautiful inscapes by the screwing up of the petals into straight little barrels or tubes" (*Notebooks,* p. 149). The distinctive design apparent to the poet must inevitably be expressed in language more sensuous and concrete than that used to posit a metaphysical mode of determination conceived by the philosopher. But this is not to say that inscape is solely pattern as perceived by the senses alone; it is a metaphysical reality as well.

The analogy with *haecceitas,* Scotus' *ultima realitas entis,* makes unmistakable the objectivity of inscape. There was considerable confusion among early critics on this point, one of them describing inscape as a "process of drawing sensuous impression inward." From all of Hopkins' remarks, however, it is clear that inscape is an objectively existing reality, the uniqueness of a being, independent of the observer. He speaks of inscape being "discovered" and of its being "buried away from simple people and yet how near at hand if they had eyes to see it" (*Notebooks,* p. 161). In what is perhaps his earliest use of the term—a college essay on Parmenides—he declares:

For the phenomenal world . . . is the brink, limbus, lapping, run-and-mingle of two principles which meet in the scape of everything—probably Being under its modification of siding, of particular oneness of Being, and Not-Being, under its siding of the Many. The two may be called two degrees of siding in the scale of Being . . . the inscape will be the proportion of the mixture.

In other words, inscape is ontological, the never-to-be-repeated "bread of being," the meeting of the One and the Many, of unity and variety in the unique object of the poet's "seeing."

With the concept of instress critics have had more difficulty than with that of inscape. Although they have made some use here also of Scotistic analogies, their definitions of instress are still not wholly satisfactory in the light of Hopkins' own use of the word. It is for him charged with significance; it expresses fundamental notions of being, and it is vital to what may be called his aesthetic epistemology. For it is, I think, as a means of perception that instress is to be understood. And Scotus

35

again offers us the tools so to understand it. If the Scotistic theory of individuation has been helpful as an analogue of inscape, the Scotistic theory of knowledge is equally helpful as a philosophic parallel to instress.

In contrast to inscape, instress appears to be not wholly objective but in some way related also to the person perceiving, to the subject. In his frequent references to instress, Hopkins emphasizes now its objective character, now its subjective, but always with the implication of something inherent in the object which is brought to its full being only in the effect upon the percipient subject. In his description of Ely Cathedral, he indicates that instress exists outside the observer and causes a reaction in him: "The all-powerfulness of instress in mode and the immediateness of its effect are very remarkable" (*Notebooks*, p. 119). The words "powerful" and "immediate" here are important, revealing the pressure of instress on the person perceiving it. The struggle to capture in words the quality of the instress he feels in the object is shown in another note:

Take a few primroses in a glass and the instress of brilliancy, sort of starriness: I have not the right word—so simple a flower gives is remarkable. It is, I think, due to the strong swell given by the deeper yellow middle [*Notebooks*, p. 142].

Again he describes the blue of the sky as "charged with simple instress, the higher, zenith sky earnest and frowning, lower more light and sweet" (*Notebooks*, p. 142). The metaphors, "strong swell," "charged," suggest surely that instress exists objectively and also that by its very nature it demands a subject, one who will feel the "swell," experience the "charge." In other references Hopkins treats instress chiefly from the point of view of the subject, as in his description of his reaction to a comet:

The comet—I have seen it at bedtime in the west, with head to the ground, white, a soft well-shaped tail, not big: I felt a certain awe and instress, a feeling of strangeness, flight (...), and of threatening [*Notebooks*, p. 198].

36

What then about the relationship between inscape and instress? It is here, I think, that criticism can benefit by turning again to Scotus. Hopkins in a highly significant note tells us explicitly that inscape and instress are closely related: "We went up to the castle but not in: standing before the gateway I had an instress which only the true old work gives from the strong and noble inscape of the pointed arch" (*Notebooks,* pp. 216-217). In the year before he had begun to read Scotus, he was analyzing the objective-subjective character of instress and speculating on individuation. He wrote in 1871:

On this walk I came to a cross road I had been at in the morning carrying in it another 'running instress.' I was surprised to recognize it and the moment I did it lost its present instress, breaking off from what had immediately gone before, and fell into the morning's. . . . And what is this running instress, so independent of at least the immediate scape of the thing, which unmistakably distinguishes and individualizes things? Not imposed outwards from the mind as for instance by melancholy or strong feeling: I can easily distinguish that instress. I think it is this same running instress by which we identify, or better, test and refuse to identify with our various suggestions the thought which has just slipped from the mind at an interruption [*Notebooks,* p. 153].

Here he is distinguishing between "true" and "false" instress, and the true is linked with individual identity, not momentary but recognizable as part of the essential being of the object of perception, the road. Every inscape will have an instress; *this* design and no other will give rise to *this* instress and no other.

Springing from the distinctiveness of the individual object, instress conveys, as it were, that distinctiveness, the *haecceitas,* to the perceiver. In other words, instress is the means by which inscape is realized by the poet. When he "takes in" any inscape, he does so because of the instress which stems from its unique being and which exerts upon him the pressure of its unique being. The relationship between the poet and what he sees is intimate, neither intellectual alone nor sensitive alone, but a commingling of both modes of knowing, a simultaneity of senses, emotion and mind. He "becomes" what he sees: the uniqueness of the object is borne in upon him by the instress carried in it, but coming to its fullest existence only in his response.

In Scotus' theory of knowledge there is a striking counterpart to such an explanation of instress. Scotus, eager to preserve a close contact between the mind and external reality, and postulating, as we have seen, as a principle of individuation a thisness not wholly material but also formal, allows preliminary and direct knowledge of the individual being of an object, before knowledge of its universal essence. In this he differs from the Thomistic position, in which Hopkins as a Jesuit was trained, and which declares in part that the intelligence can know, at first hand, only the universal by its abstraction from the particular, and that knowledge of the particular, the concrete, can reach the mind only by a process known as "conversion." But Scotus describes a "first act" in which the intelligence and the senses, acting simultaneously, grasp the immediate reality of the concrete, singular object. This first act is intuitive, neither intellectual only nor sensitive only, but both at once (*Op. Ox.*, I, d. iii, qu. 2, 8). Such a compound of what for the Scholastics are two distinct modes of epistemological relationship: the knowledge of the intellect, which being immaterial can know only form, and perception by the senses, which being material are aware only of the concrete—such a compound is made possible by Scotus' defining the ultimate determination of the being, its *haecceitas,* as proper neither to matter alone nor to form alone, but to both. This point is of importance in the analogies I have described with inscape and instress.

Critics like Christopher Devlin [3] and, later, W. H. Gardner [4] have recognized the similarity of Scotus' "first act" of knowing to Hopkins' instress, although none of them has pursued the analogy to any point where it may shed light on a concept which is so fundamental to Hopkins' aesthetic theory. If, as we have seen, inscape is the objectively-existing individuality of an object and as such is related to Scotus' *haecceitas,* and instress is the quasi-objective quality of *distinctiveness as it is perceived by the observer,* and as such is related to Scotus' "first act" of knowledge, is it then possible by investigating Scotus further, to discover anything more specific about the relationship between inscape and instress? I think that it is.

According to Scotus, direct knowledge of the individual concrete is made possible by the existence in the object of a multiplicity of distinct metaphysical entities, which he calls *formalitates.* These are *formalitates a parte rei,* that is, grounded in the objective nature of reality itself, and in their variety and wealth constituting the individuality of the object, the *haecceitas* perceived in the first act of knowledge. The *formalitates,* however, as modifications of individual being, are only partial and incomplete and are completed and fulfilled in the intuitive act by which the intellect and the senses simultaneously react to them, thereby "knowing" the uniqueness, the distinctiveness of the object (*Op. Ox.,* d. iii, qu. 2, n. 26; qu. 6, 15). In other words, the *formalitates* are a bridge between essential individuality and the mind and senses perceiving it.

Scotus' theories of *haecceitas,* the *formalitates,* and the *primum actum* of knowledge, thus related, can now be seen as remarkable philosophic counterparts to Hopkins' ideas of inscape and instress, which are primarily aesthetic. Our understanding of the concept of instress, particularly is clarified when instress is regarded in the light of the *formalitates,* as a principle of pressure existing in the inscape by virtue of its distinctiveness, conveying to the immediate perception of the poet the very being of that distinctiveness, and being experienced by him as an aesthetic intuition with all its force and excitement.

But indeed I have often felt when I have been in this mood and felt the depth of an instress or how fast the inscape holds a thing that nothing is so pregnant to the truth as simple yes and *is*. There would be no bridge, no stem of stress between us and things to bear us out and carry the mind over. . . . [*Notebooks*, p. 98].

There the thing *is*, *this* thing and no other, and by our intuitive awareness of its uniqueness we know its essential being, not by abstraction, but immediately.

It is because I feel that Hopkins, growing more aware after 1872 of his affinities with Scotus, must have attached to instress a meaning very like that of the *formalitates* and the first act of knowledge that I take issue with Father Peters on some points.

The double aspect of objectivity-subjectivity in instress that I have already pointed out is also apparent to Father Peters. He feels that instress

stands for two distinct and separate things, related to each other as cause and effect; as a cause 'instress' refers for Hopkins to that core of being or inherent energy which is the actuality of the object; as effect 'instress' stands for the specifically individual impression the object makes on man [p. 15].

While it is true that instress means under its objective aspect the core of being which is the actuality of the object, it must be particularly emphasized that for Hopkins, as for Scotus, the core is a core of individuality, the actuality is a distinctive and unique actuality, and instress in some way constitutes that uniqueness, as the *formalitates* are the metaphysical basis of *haecceitas*. It is thus that the instress felt by the poet is a response to uniqueness and to immediate and concrete reality. No two distinct and separate things, but one relationship, instress is the bridge between inscape and the poet.

Father Peters says further, "We observe that in the act of perception inscape is known first, and in this grasp of the inscape is felt the stress of being behind it, is felt its instress" (p. 14). From none of his own examples nor from any others I have found in Hopkins can Father Peters, I think, support the statement that inscape is "known first." If the analogy with Scotus' *haecceitas* is a valid one, and Father Peters thinks it is, then the stress of being is not "behind" the inscape, but is identical with it. And it is this stress of being which is intuitively perceived by the poet. "I saw the inscape, though freshly, as if my eyes were still growing, though with a companion the eye and the ear are for the most part shut and instress cannot come" (*Notebooks*, p. 171). The crux of the matter lies in Father Peters' definition of inscape as a "sensitive manifestation of a being's individuality" (p. 14). It thus, he says, must be "perceived by the senses, but instress, though given in the perception of inscape, is not directly perceived by the senses, because it is not a primary sensible quality of the thing" (p. 14). This insistence on inscape as merely sensible inevitably leads to a distorted understanding of instress. Inscape as a complex of sense-data may seem plausible at first when one reads Hopkins' descriptions of inscape in nature, "sea and sky," but immediately upon awareness of how much further he carries the concept in his concern with human beings, and with art, follows the necessary recognition of inscape as involving much more than the senses alone. The concept of inscape underlies all his emphasis on the *self*, of others and his own, in poems like *Felix Randall* and *Harry Ploughman*, "world's loveliest—men's selves," and in all the sonnets so profoundly concerned with "this poor Jackself." Obviously the inscape of a man cannot be found only in what is perceptible to the senses alone, but also in what is the chief pitch of his being for Hopkins, his soul.

And so with the inscape of a poem. Hopkins calls inscape the "essential and only lasting thing" in poetry, and the mass of evidence Father Peters has accumulated to show how he applied this canon to his own work and to that of others is unanswerable testimony to the more-than-sensible nature of inscape. The poetic experience is surely intuitive, a compound of senses and emotion and mind, and the poem an organic expression of all these. Poetry for Hopkins is "speech for the inscape's sake."

Inscape, then, whether it be of a flower, a scene in Wales, one of Purcell's airs, or a boy bugler, is the "bead of being," is "rarest-veined" reality, and it is perceived not by the poet's senses alone, but by the whole man in an immediate, intuitive act. And when each mortal thing "deals" out that being indoors each one dwells," it does so by means of the instress which is the core of that being, and which exerts its pressure on the mind and senses of the person intuiting it.

Austin Warren's remark that, since inscape is so central a word in Hopkins' vocabulary and a motif in his mental life, it "moves through some range of meaning, from sense-perceived pattern to inner form," [5] is only an approximation of the more precise meaning which the analogy with *haecceitas* shows that inscape most probably has. Just because they are so central to Hopkins' sensibility, neither inscape nor instress "move through" a range of meaning. When inscape is considered in close conjunction with instress (and when Scotus' *haecceitas* and his intuitive, intellectual-sensitive first act of knowledge are remembered), it is clear how inscape can be grasped as sense-perceived pattern and inner form *at one and the same time.*

Hopkins' ideas of inscape and instress were clear and distinct and already the center of his aesthetic life long before he knew Scotus' commentary on the *Sentences*. What relations, therefore, that exist between inscape and *haecceitas* and between instress and the *formalitates* and the *primum actum* are analogies rather than identities. Nonetheless there is no question that Scotus was a strong influence in clarifying and supporting Hopkins' ideas. Only one thoroughly familiar, perhaps, with the somewhat remote position assigned to the particular in the Thomistic theory of knowledge can fully grasp the excitement of the Scotistic divergence. Hopkins by virtue of his training as a Jesuit was keenly aware of the difference. Immediate contact with the myriad distinctive and unique beings of the external world seems to be at the very heart of the aesthetic experience. Hence Hopkins' flash of enthusiasm on finding in Scotus a kindred spirit, full of concern for the unique individual, dealing with metaphysics, true, but in every line enlarging and validating an aesthetic theory already subtle and penetrating.

NOTES

1 W. A. M. Peters, S.J., *Gerard Manley Hopkins* (London: Oxford University Press, 1948).

2 G. F. Lahey, S.J., *The Life of Father Gerard Manley Hopkins* (London: Oxford University Press, 1930), p. 129.

3 "Hopkins and Duns Scotus," *New Verse*, XIV (1935), 13-14.

4 W. H. Gardner (ed.), *Gerard Manley Hopkins* (London: Martin Secker and Warburg, 1944), I, 22-28.

5 "Instress of Inscape," Kenyon Critics (ed.), *Gerard Manley Hopkins* (Norfolk, Conn.: New Directions Press, 1945), p. 77.

M. B. McNamee, S.J.

MASTERY AND MERCY IN

THE WRECK OF THE DEUTSCHLAND

I think it will be readily admitted that what constitutes a truly religious poet is the degree in which his poetry is suffused with the truths of the supernatural. Religious poetry is poetry written by a poet to whom the truths of the order of grace have become so second nature that they pervade his every thought as the soul pervades the body. If this be granted, then there is no poet in the English language who is more fundamentally and persistently religious than Gerard Manley Hopkins. Some aspect of the supernatural is part of almost every poem he wrote. The beauty and lovableness of God communicated through the "pied" beauty of His creation, the mystery of the Incarnation, the Pauline doctrine of the Mystical Body of Christ, the mysterious workings of God's grace in the hearts of men, and the unique place of Mary as Mediatrix of all Graces in the economy of Salvation—these are the ever recurring themes of Hopkins' poetry. They are not mere intermittent references, not mere occasional allusions; they pervade his poetry from beginning to end. Take them away and there is little of thematic value left.

Another facet of Hopkins thinking and experience as a religious poet that is almost as pervasive in his poetry as these general religious truths is the logical and psychological impact of *The Spiritual Exercises of Saint Ignatius*. [1] Individual exercises of the Ignatian retreat provide the theme and create the tone of many of his shorter poems, but his most sustained poetic effort, *The Wreck of the Deutschland*, gives poetic expression to the whole of *The Exercises*. It is the entire logical and psychological sweep of *The Exercises* that colors both the theme of the whole poem and very especially the thought and emotional progression of part one. It is my purpose here, by a careful analysis of part one and the pertinent lines of part two, to show what the poem owes to Hopkins' deep understanding and appreciation of *The Spiritual Exercises*. How completely Hopkins understood *The Exercises* of Saint Ignatius is revealed by his penetrating commentary on them which has been recently published.

In the briefest possible descriptive statement, *The Spiritul Exercises* of Saint Ignatius might be said to progress logically from a realization of the mastery of God over the individual soul by reason of the fact that He created it to an ever deepening appreciation of the mercy and love of God for the individual soul manifested in the Incarnation, the Passion, Death, and Resurrection of Christ, King and Savior. Psychologically, the realization of the mastery of God the Creator evokes in the human soul a sense of reverential awe of God and a sense of dependence upon Him; while the appreciation of the utter selfless love and boundless mercy of Christ the Redeemer elicits a return of unselfish, generous love. The main motivation of *The Exercises,* then, might be summed up as the majesty of God the Creator inducing a reverence and awe for Him as Lord and Master and the mercy and love of Christ the Redeemer instilling in the hearts of men a generous and unselfish service of Christ the King.

It is my contention that it is this logical and psychological progression of *The Exercises* that determines both the theme of the whole *Wreck of the Deutschland* and its thought and emotional progress. The theme of the whole poem might be stated thus: It is only humble submission to the will of God, our Creator and Lord, and an unselfish love of Christ, our King and Redeemer, that give meaning to life and that enable one to understand and joyfully accept the hard things in life along with the pleasant. In developing that theme the poet divides his poem into two main parts. Part one elaborates the principles of the spiritual life as the poet himself came to understand them, and part two gives a dramatic example of the effects of these principles on the life of individuals who have learned to live by them—(the nuns in the wreck and especially the "tall" nun) and upon those with whom they come in contact (the rest of the passengers on board the Deutschland, the "comfortless unconfessed of them").

We are sure that Hopkins had his own spiritual experience in mind in the poem because he tells us so. In a letter to Robert Bridges in which he mentions the poem, he says: "I may add for your greater interest and edification that what refers to myelf in the poem is all strictly and literally true and did all occur. Nothing is added for poetical padding." [2] When he wrote the poem, he had been in the Society of Jesus for several years. He had made the thirty-eight day retreat built on *The Exercises* each year after his novitiate, and had meditated their truths for an hour each morning. It should not be surprising, then, to discover that, when he came to write his great poem commemorating the five Sisters drowned in the wreck of the Deutschland, the principles of successful Christian living were central to his thought, that those principles as outlined by Saint Ignatius were foremost in his consciousness, and that they colored his generalizations on the spiritual life in part one and even the narrative of the wreck in part two.

A careful reading of part one does reveal, in fact, a thought and emotional progress almost identical to that of *The Spiritual Exercises*. It begins with the notion of the mastery of God the Creator, "thou mastering me God, giver of breath and bread," and works through a feeling of almost terrifying awe at the greatness of God, "and after it almost unmade, what with dread, Thy doing," to a sense of the mercy and love of Christ, manifested in His Incarnation, in His suffering and death, and, mysteriously, in the very sacrifices demanded by the stress and storms of life. And God is finally seen not merely as a

Master but also as a lover, Who may demand sacrifices but a lover still. He is "lightning and love"; He is a father who must be cruel only to be kind—a "father and fondler of a heart thou hast wrung." Part one ends sounding the two notes which together create the basis for the harmony of the whole *Spiritual Exercises*—mastery and mercy, the mastery of God the Creator and the mercy and love of Christ the Redeemer.

> Make mercy in all of us, out of us all.
> Mastery, but be adored, but be adored King.

These same notes are sounded again in the recapitulation at the end of part two, where we find the poet admiring the "master of the tides," the very "ground of being, and granite of it: past all grasp God," but also the "Mercy that outrides the all of water," "Our passion-plunged giant risen, the Christ of the Father compassionate, fetched in the storm of his strides." The whole poem ends where *The Exercises* end on a note of triumph, sounding the hope of a resurrection—"Let Him easter in us, be a dayspring to the dimness of us, be a crimson-cresseted east." And the very last line of all gives final and magnificent voice to the two dominant notes that have sounded over and over again throughout the poem as they do throughout *The Exercises*—mastery and love. In the phrase "Our hearts' charity's hearth's fire," the note of love is sounded for the last time, and, in "our thoughts' chivalry's throng's Lord," the note of mastery. The mastery of God the Creator over the creature He has made *is* the bed-rock, granite foundation of the spiritual life and of *The Spiritual Exercises*. It opens Hopkins' poem ("Thou *mastering* me God!"); it concludes part one ("out of us all Mastery, but be adored, but be adored *King*"); and it creates the finale of part two as well (our thoughts' chivalry's throng's *Lord*"). I do not think that it is forcing things to see an influence of *The Spiritual Exercises* on this general thought and emotional progress of the poem. A more careful, stanza by stanza, analysis, however, will reveal even more clearly how much the poem owes to Hopkins' deep insights into the spirit and movement of *The Exercises*.

We have seen that the fact of creation and all that it implies of man's relationship to God, his Lord and Master, is the foundation of the whole *Spiritual Exercises* of Saint Ignatius. It is that fact and its consequences to which Hopkins gives beautiful expression in the first stanzas of part one. This idea is given its strongest expression in the opening verse: "Thou mastering me God." The realization that God, as Creator, is my master and I am His servant are the two most essential principles of progress in the spiritual life. In a letter to Reverend Urquhart, whom he was trying to convert to Catholicism, Hopkins once said: "Until you prefer God to the world and yourself, you have not made the first step." The spiritual life is an eminently personal relationship between the individual human soul and God and therefore *the* most important implication in the notion of creation is that God created *me* and is, therefore, *my* Master. ("Thou mastering *me* God.") Hopkins keeps the light of his poetry focused on the first person pronoun in these stanzas: "mastering *me*," "Thou hast bound bones and veins in *me*, fastened *me* flesh," "dost thou touch *me* afresh?" "over again I feel thy finger," "I did say yes," "Thou heardest *me* truer than tongue confess."

Along with this recognition of personal dependence upon God and His mastery of *me*, iterated again and again in these stanzas, goes the equally important recognition that God is master of all things else on the face of the earth because He has also made them, and that He made them for *me*. All these things are His gifts to me to help me on my way: God is the "giver of breath and bread"—of life and of the means of sustaining it. Here Hopkins is still on the personal—*my* life and the means of sustaining it. But in the next verse his vision fans out to embrace the notion of God as master of the whole vast world which I inhabit, both land and sea, "world's strand, sway of the sea." The word "sway" especially prevents us from neglecting the focal point of God's mastery of the world He has created. But God's mastery over the men He has created to populate the world is not limited by time; it also sweeps out into eternity; it embraces all men, living and dead; God is "Lord of living and dead." But as important as is God's mastery of the whole of creation and of all human beings, *the* important realization for *me* is that He is *my* master because He made *me*. Therefore, Hopkins reverts to that essential notion in verse five where he reiterates in fresh and graphic terms the fact that God made me. "Thou hast bound bones and veins in *me*, fastened *me* flesh."

The concept of creation is so difficult that a clear idea of it has never been arrived at independent of revelation. It is no wonder, then, that, when it is first seen in all its overwhelming implications, it induces a sense of awe which is almost akin to terror. Many spiritual writers have spoken of this sense of well-nigh annihilating terror that fills the soul when the full impact of the Creator's majesty and the creature's nothingness first sweeps in upon it. Much of the first part of *The Spiritual Exercises* is devoted to making the retreatant sense this abyss that exists between himself and God. Hopkins expresses that feeling in the verse: "And after it [after making me] almost unmade, what with dread, Thy doing." But this very sense of awe and dread is a grace from God, impressing on the creature his utter nothingness in himself and his complete dependence upon God for his very being. This is the true basis of humility. Hopkins saw that realization as a great grace and was ready to welcome whatever graces succeeded it. He borrows words from Saint Paul here to describe the action of God's grace upon his soul. In his *Comments on The Spiritual Exercises of Saint Ignatius* he describes grace as lifting "the receiver from one cleave of being to another and to a vital act in Christ: this is truly God's finger touching the very vein of personality." [3] These comments were written much later than *The Wreck,* but, here, in stanza one, we already hear him speaking of a visitation of grace as the finger of God: "and dost thou touch me afresh? Over again I feel thy finger and find thee."

The acknowledgment of God's supreme mastery and our nothingness is hard on human nature; it is hard on human pride. Its logical necessity is inescapable, but that does not make the naked surrender of the soul to God anything but, at first, terrifying. Hopkins describes his own surrender to God his Creator, and the awesome fear that accompanied it in the second stanza. "I did say yes" —there is the surrender; but it is a surrender to a God Who seems all terrifying power and majesty: "I did say yes, O at *lightning* and *lashed rod.*" Both lightning and the lashed rod of a master are symbols of God's overpowering might and majesty. In the presence of God, truthfully conceived, terror and fear are natural. "Thou heardst me truer than tongue confess Thy terror, O Christ, O God." (It may not be accidental, and even if it is, it is still appropriate, that the term "Christ," which means the annointed one of God, one, therefore, having the complete authority of God, rather than "Jesus," which means "Savior," is used here where it is Christ the Judge that is thought of rather than Christ, the Merciful Redeemer. Later in stanza 30, where it is the mercy and love of Christ that is being emphasized, "Jesu" is used.) Verses five to eight of this stanza merely localize and further circumstance the poet's surrender to the terrifying truth of the allness of God and his own nothingness. He made his surrender at night in a chapel before the Blessed Sacrament, "Thou knowest the walls, altar and hour and night." But more important than place and time are the unforgettable circumstances of the first complete surrender to God. The sweeping vision of the immensity of God and his own puniness in contrast almost caused him to swoon in terror at the abyss which separates him as creature from his Creator. "The swoon of a heart that the sweep and the hurl of thee trod/ /Hard down with a horror of height." It is as if he were almost swept off his feet in an effort to stand up against the hurl of the vision of God's greatness pressing upon him; every fiber of his being is astrain in the effort not to be trodden down by the towering sweep of the vision, by the "horror of height." It is as if he were almost swept off his feet in an effort to stand up against the hurl of the vision of God's greatness pressing upon him; every fiber of his being is astrain in the effort not to be trodden down by the towering sweep of the vision, by the "horror of height." "And the midriff astrain with leaning." And at the same time he is putting forth every effort to make his surrender to the compelling power of God. "Laced with [bound with] fire of stress [a grace driving him on to make his surrender in spite of his horror of height]." Hopkins frequently uses "fire" or "flame" to signify the operations of divine grace. Thus in his diary he says: "All things therefore are charged with God and if we know how to touch them give off sparks and take fire" (N., p. 342). Thus here, although it almost tears him apart to do it, the fire of God's grace enables him to make the surrender.

Once the fact of God's mastery and the soul's dependence upon God is apprehended, St. Ignatius insists, there is no possible choice for the rational being except total surrender to the will of God, terrifying though that surrender may seem to weak human nature. The refusal to make this surrender, the refusal to submit to God, is sin. It was the original sin and it is every personal sin as well. And the ultimate fatal consequence of sin is Hell— eternal separation from the God whom the sinner has stubbornly refused to serve. It is either, then, God or Hell. That is the frightening alternative set before us in St. Ignatius' meditation on Hell in *The Spiritual Exercises.* It is the alternative confronting the poet, too, in the first verses of stanza three: "The frown of his face/ /Before me"—the mastering God, who seems to demand so much, on the one hand; and, on the other, "the hurtle of hell/ /Behind." The confusion of the soul confronted with these fearsome alternatives is caught in the very broken movement itself of verse three. Where was the poet to turn? "where, where was a, where was a place?" There is no doubt. In such a dilemma, there is nothing to do but make a complete and unconditional surrender to God. The poet rejoices now that he had the courage to make a complete and unconditional surrender to God. The poet rejoices now that he had the courage to make that capitulation. In one magnanimous gesture he yielded his will totally to the will of God. He dramatizes that surrender in an apostrophe to his own heart, the traditional symbol of the will. In a striking metaphor he calls it a carrier-pigeon, which, when released, flies straight and unswervingly to its home. The poet's home is the "heart of the Host," the Heart of Christ, beating for him in the Holy Eucharist. The surrender, then, turns out to be not as terrifying as it seemed at first; it is, after all, a heart speaking to a heart. Already some of the fearsomeness of the capitulation is melting.

> I whirled out wings that spell on that occasion
> And fled with a fling of the heart to the heart
> of the Host.

Surprisingly enough, the surrender, that looked so frightening in prospect, in actuality brings an immediate feeling of exhilaration and singular achievement. The poet congratulates his heart because it was so "dovewinged" —so rightly affectioned, so "carrier-witted"—so right-minded, so set on its proper home, that it cooperated so fully with the grace of God as to make this total capitulation to His will—"To flash from the flame to the flame then, tower from the grace to the grace." Here "flame" is explicitly identified with grace. It is in apposition to "grace" in the phrase "tower from the grace to the grace." The surrender to this first great searing but enflaming grace of God enkindles others, through which one can tower from one spiritual height to another.

This kind of achievement is a thing almost entirely of

the inmost soul. It is not a thing that creates a great stir in the world; it may not be known to any save God and the individual soul itself. As unspectacular as it may appear to men, it is an achievement made possible only by the supernatural grace of God. For a man to see that this *is* where real achievement lies, he needs the light of faith to correct his natural myopia which sees achievement only in flashy external exploits. This is a fundamental truth of the spiritual life which Hopkins refers to in two striking images in stanza four. The cataclysmic struggle which has been going on in his soul, and which he recreates in stanzas one and three, precisely because it is interior, is totally invisible to others about him. He is like sand in an hourglass. Look at the glass obliquely and nothing at all seems to be happening in it. It presents a bland, unruffled appearance; but look at it from above and it is seen to be positively mined with motion. The grains of sand that looked so immobile when seen obliquely are almost all in motion and are crowding one another and drifting to the point where they fall through to the compartment below. That is the way the poet is—calm on the surface, but alive with intensest spiritual activity within, unnoticed obliquely by men, but seen from above by God.

> I am soft sift
> In an hour glass—at the wall
> Fast, but mined with a motion, a drift,
> And it crowds and it combs to the fall.

Or he is like water in a well. Look at the surface of a spring fed by an underground stream, and it is perfectly placid and calm. You would never suspect the vigorous rush of the mountain stream that feeds it. So, too, the poet, placid and calm on the surface, as placid and unruffled as a pane of glass, is driven by all the compulsion of the principle of God's mastery over his soul and by the pressure of the grace of Christ fed down to him by the stream of revelation, "a vein of the gospel proffer."

> I steady as a water in a well, to a poise,
>   to a pane,
> But roped with [bound with], always, all
>   the way down from the tall
> Fells or flanks of the voel [a mountain
>   stream], a vein
> Of the gospel proffer, a pressure, a
>   principle, Christ's gift.

But the spiritual life, Saint Ignatius makes clear in *The Spiritual Exercises,* is not to be built merely on the compulsion of the foundation of God's mastery over the creature of His hands, or even merely upon the revelation which He makes of Himself in the mystery of the Incarnation. This creates a new foundation and establishes forever a new principle—the principle and foundation of love and mercy. The Incarnation throws a new light on the whole universe; it can no longer be seen just as a reflection of the Creator's beauty and power; it must also be seen to reflect His love and mercy. That is the new foundation upon which the exercises of the second and third parts of *The Spiritual Exercises* are built, and it is a truth which affected Hopkins profoundly. The whole universe has been transformed by the Incarnation. The beauty and the splendor of the material world has been elevated because the Son of God has assumed from it a material, body; and suffering and death have finally taken on new meaning and value because the Son of God made man has endured them and given them sacrificial value. The poet now sees not only the beauty and majesty of God the Creator manifested in creation but also the love of the Father made known to him through His Son Incarnate.

All the "terror" and the "horror of height" give way now to a familiar greeting between friends. The poet represents himself as kissing his hand in greeting to God wafted to him out of the beauty of stars or out of a dappled-with-damson sunset sky. The very word "wafted" connotes a gentle, loving manifestation free of all the overpowering awesomeness of stanza two. Or in another mood, the poet can glow in the glory of the God of thunder.

> I kiss my hand
> To the stars, lovely-asunder
> Starlight, wafting him out of it; and
> Glow, glory in thunder;
> Kiss my hand to the dappled-with-damson west.

The God of power and majesty is still a fact; God is still "under the splendour and wonder," but a much more compelling fact to the poet now is the *mystery* of God, the astounding fact of the Incarnation which completely transforms everything in time, both its joys and sorrows. "His mystery must be instressed, stressed." The mystery, central to Hopkins' thinking and central to the rest of the poem, is the mystery of the Incarnation with all that it implies of sacrificial love. It must be instressed, i.e., it must be made real to us; it must be stressed, i.e., the knowledge of the mystery of God Incarnate and its consequences must be brought to fruition in our souls. When I understand the full significance of that mystery, I see Christ in every aspect of life and bless Him in His unpleasant as well as in His pleasant visitations. "For I greet him the days I meet him, and bless when I understand." And it takes the impact of the Incarnation to enable me to see God in the hard things of life. To see Christ in the whole of life is a difficult lesson to learn. We do not see Him now as He is in His beatific bliss; He is made known to us only indirectly through things that seem to have no connection with Heaven at all ("nor first from heaven") in the stress of stars or the stroke of storms. Few know the mysterious fact that it is in these very things that Christ visits us and enables us to realize the stress of divine grace in our lives.

> Not out of his bliss
> Springs the stress felt

Nor first from heaven (and few know this)
Swings the stroke dealt—
Stroke and a stress that stars and storms
       deliver,
That guilt is hushed by, hearts are flushed
       by and melt.

In the presence of these mysterious visitations of grace, and especially by the advent of Christ in the storms of life, the guilty are often hushed in fear—the guilty whom nothing else in life has disturbed; but devoted hearts are often melted in a true spirit of self-immolating love.

But though there may be few who really know the mystery of the Incarnation and the transformation it works on the joys and sufferings of life, it is the most central and the most enduring fact of time. "It rides time like riding a river." A remark which Hopkins makes in his *Commentary on the Exercises* may help to interpret this verse. "Time has three dimensions and one positive pitch or direction. It is therefore not so much like any river or sea as like the Sea of Galilee, which has the Jordan running through it and giving a current to the whole" (N., p. 343). This note was written in 1881 during Hopkins' Long Retreat in the Tertianship, many years after *The Wreck;* but, judging from the manner in which other images and allusions keep recurring in his writings over long periods of years, it may not be farfetched to suggest that what he states explicitly here was in his mind when he wrote this verse some years previously in *The Wreck*. If so, the verse would mean that the Mystery of the Incarnation with all its implications of sacrificial love rides time like a riding river, like the river Jordan riding the Sea of Galilee and giving a current to the whole. The Incarnation runs through time as through a lake and gives a forever new direction and current to everything in time —both its joys and its sorrows. This is a staggering fact, the poet says, even to the faithful—"the faithless fable and miss."

Hopkins implies in *The Wreck* and states elsewhere that

the Incarnation is the central fact of history; that it splits time in two; and that it alone gives true meaning to life and to life's sorrows. After the Incarnation, he says, nothing in life can ever again be trivial because God has shared it all with us. That is why every moment of the life of the God Incarnate, from Galilee to Calvary, is worth meditating and is meditated in the third and fourth parts of *The Spiritual Exercises*. It is the Incarnation and its transformation of all of life and especially of its sufferings into a sacrifice of love that also come to the fore in stanzes seven and eight of *The Wreck*.

> It dates from day
> Of his going in Galilee;
> Warm-laid grave of a womb-life grey.

The life of the Second Person of the Blessed Trinity in His assumed nature in the womb of His Mother was like being alive in a dark grave compared to the blazing light of His life in the bosom of the Trinity. But the Son of God deliberately assumed with His human nature all the limitations of that nature to be able to sacrifice Himself for us—the poverty of Bethlehem, the long years of dependence upon His Mother for the necessities of life ("maiden's knee"), the terrible humiliation and sufferings of His agony and death ("the dense and the driven Passion, and frightful sweat"). And as a result of His assumption of the limitations of human nature and deliberate choice of suffering and death, the current of human life itself and of human hardships and sufferings forever swell into new meaning and value which were only faintly guessed at before and never fully realized.

> Thence the discharge of it, there its
> swelling to be
> Though felt before, though in high flood
> yet—
> What none would have known of it.

In fact, the poet feels that it is only when a person is pushed into a corner by a reversal of some kind that he shows whether he has grasped the full import of the mystery of the Incarnation or not, whether he can see Christ in the storms of life as well as in the stars and sunsets.

> . . . only the heart being hard at bay
> **Is out with it.**

Man, in these circumstances, is like an animal at bay. If it is in good fettle, it will show the advantage as it lashes out at its foe; if it is not, it will show up badly.

> We lash with the best or worst word last!

If we have assimilated the full meaning of the Incarnation and see the sacrificial value it gives to all reversals, we will accept them lovingly; we will lash with our best word last; we will say "yes, oh at lightning and lashed rod"; but, if we have not inscaped suffering with the suffering Christ, then we will lash with our worst word last —a word of rebellion against suffering and the God Who permits it.

The taste of suffering is like the taste of a sloe. If the sloe is ripe, we are suffused with sweetness; if it is not ripe, we are puckered up with sourness. If we inscape our suffering with Christ, Our Suffering Lord and Redeemer, it fills us with sweetness, the sweetness of a sacrifice made for one we love; if we do not so inscape it, it puckers us to the roots of our souls with its bitterness. Hopkins' lines themselves are here suffused with the sweetness of the ripe sloe and puckered with the sourness of the green one.

> How a lush-kept plush-capped sloe
> Will, mouthed to flesh-burst,
> Gush!—flush the man, the being with it,
>   sour or sweet,
> Brim, in a flash, full!

But whether one acknowledges Christ, God-made-man, the hero of Calvary, in life or not, the poet continues, all men will have to acknowledge Him in the end, when they appear before Him as their Judge. Whether they intended to go there, whether they want to, whether they were warned about this eventuality or not, in the end, all paths will meet at the "hero of Calvary, Christ's feet." Whether they receive a loving welcome or a condemnation from Christ their King and Judge will depend upon whether they welcomed or rejected Him during life.

> Hither, then, last or first
> To hero of Calvary, Christ's feet,
> Never ask if meaning it, wanting it,
> warned of it, men go.

Finally, as in the coda of a symphony, Hopkins recapitulates the two familiar themes—God's mastery and mercy. In a direct prayer to the Triune God, first His mastery is acknowledged.

> Be adored among men,
> God, three-numbered form;
> Wring thy rebel, dogged in den,
> Man's malice, with wrecking and storm.

It may take this kind of God-handling to bring rebellious man to bow to God; but, when he does, he discovers the mysterious antinomy of God's ways—that He is both a Master and a Lover.

> Beyond saying sweet, past telling of
> tongue,
> Thou art lightning and love, I found
> it, a winter and warm;
>
> Father and fondler of heart thou hast
> wrung:
> Hast thy dark descending and most art
> merciful then.

In the light of this vision of God's strange ways with the hearts of men, the poet ends part one with a direct petition that God make His will prevail in the lives of all men. Let Him take man's heart by violence if necessary. And here the poet's language echoes that of John Donne in "Batter my heart, three-personed God."

> With an anvil-ding
> And with fire in him forge thy will.

Or He may achieve His will with man by stealing into his heart like a gentle spring breeze.

> Or rather, rather then, stealing as Spring
> Through him, melt him but master him still.

He took the first way with Paul on the road to Damascus; the latter with Augustine for whose conversion Saint Monica prayed for nineteen years.

> Whether at once, as once at a crash Paul,
> Or as Austin, a lingering-out sweet skill.

But however it be accomplished, at a crash or by slow attrition, the one thing vital in life, the poet insists, is that God's mercy and mastery prevail.

> Make mercy in all of us, out of us all
> Mastery, but be adored, but be adored King.

In part two of the poem Hopkins illustrates, in the conduct of the "tall nun" and her companions in the wreck, the singleness of vision that these principles provide a person who lives by them. Because she has learned to see Christ in the storms of life as well as in its pleasures, her first and only thought in the brawling of the storm was of Christ her Master.

> *Ipse* the only one, Christ, King, Head:
> He was to cure the extremity where he
>   had cast her;
> Do, deal, lord it with living and dead;
> Let him ride, her pride, in his triumph,
>   despatch and have done with his doom
>   there.

Because her heart was so right and her eye so single, she could read "the unshapeable shock night,/ /And knew the who and the why." And because she herself could see so clearly Christ coming in the strides of the storm, she, in turn, became a "blown beacon of light," a means of hope, grace, and salvation to the rest on board the doomed Deutschland, to "the comfortless unconfessed of them." And thus Christ's mercy and mastery reached all on board, and the shipwreck was a harvest and the tempest carried grain. Christ came to them.

> Not a dooms-day dazzle in his coming
>   nor dark as he came;
> Kind, but royally reclaiming his own;
> A released shower, let flash to the shire,
> Not a lightning of fire hard-hurled.

Kind but royally, lightning but also a released shower; here again are the familiar antinomies in Christ who is lightning and love, a winter and warm, father and fondler of heart He has wrung, Who has His dark descending but most is merciful then. It is the antinomy of mastery and mercy that weave like a leitmotif through this whole poem as they do through the whole *Spiritual Exercises* of Saint Ignatius.

NOTES

1 David A. Downes in *Gerard Manley Hopkins: A Study of His Ignatian Spirit* (Toronto: Burns & MacEachern, 1959), pp. 52-72, discusses some elements of *The Exercises* in *The Wreck*.

2 Claude C. Abbott (ed.), *The Letters of Gerard Manley Hopkins to Robert Bridges* (London: Oxford University Press, 1935), p. 47.

3 Humphry House (ed.), *The Note-books and Papers of Gerard Manley Hopkins* (London: Oxford University Press, 1937), p. 337. Future page references to the *Note-books* will be given in the text after the quotations under the designation N.

William D. Templeman

HOPKINS AND WHITMAN:

EVIDENCE OF INFLUENCE AND ECHOES

". . . I always knew in my heart Walt Whitman's mind to be more like my own. . . ." (Hopkins, in a letter to Bridges)

I

When Robert Bridges, writing to his friend Gerard Manley Hopkins, suggested that the poetry of Whitman had been influential on "The Leaden Echo" and "The Golden Echo," he raised an issue that according to Eleanor Ruggles "remains unsolved and provocative." [1] Terence Heywood, reporting his investigation of the literary ancestry of Hopkins, included consideration of Whitman as possible ancestor, but found no direct evidence of influence. At the end he declared:

And so we find that Hopkins, like most revolutionaries, instead of breaking with tradition altogether, only went back to earlier traditions; learned from (I do not mean merely knew) a greater variety of poets and languages than any English poet before him, some of which poets he in certain ways resembled, and others not; and that there are also resemblances between him and certain poets who never actually influenced him, or whom he had never heard of. The mature Hopkins had so thoroughly assimilated his influences that they emerged as echoes. . . . [2]

I intend briefly to reopen the case, and to submit evidence that some influence by Whitman upon Hopkins did emerge as echoes; and to point out some echoes in the form of parallelism, at the least.

First of all, we should like to know of any evidence of Hopkins' having read poetry by Whitman, what he read, and when. His prose remains, in various parts, provide some information, in addition to what his poetry may reveal. In 1864 he wrote to his friend Baillie: "I have written a thing I may send you called Grass Is My Garland." [3] Abbott, editor of the pertinent volume of letters, states that this has not been found among the early poems, [4] and W. H. Gardner in his 1948 edition of Hopkins' *Poems* has no further information about it. But Hopkins possibly could have remembered a suggestion or stimulus from Whitman's *Leaves of Grass* for this early thing, and so this thing not found among the extant early poems could have formed a basis for Hopkins' 1887 sonnet "Harry Ploughman." Indeed, Robert Bridges' note on this poem prints the following from a letter written by him to Hopkins:

I have been touching up some old sonnets you have never seen and have within a few days done the whole of one ... a direct picture of a ploughman, without afterthought. But when you read it let me know if there is anything like it in Walt Whitman; as perhaps there may be, and I should be sorry for that. [5]

Possibly Hopkins had striven to eradicate echoes of Whitman that he was definitely aware existed in the earlier, now lost version, echoes that might have seemed to him too obviously indicated as such by the Whitman-like title "Grass Is My Garland."

Certainly he had long been familiar with lines by Whitman glorifying grass, lines that had appeared in *Leaves of Grass* essentially the same since 1855:

A child said, *What is the grass?* fetching it to me
with full hands;
How could I answer the child? I do not know what
it is, any more than he.
I guess it must be the flag of my disposition, out
of hopeful green stuff woven.
Or I guess it is the handkerchief of the Lord,

> A scented gift and remembrancer, designedly dropt,
> Bearing the owner's name someway in the corners, that
> we may see and remark, and say, Whose? [6]

I say that Hopkins had long been familiar with these lines, for he alluded out of his memory in 1882 specifically to the figure of the handkerchief of the Lord, a gift and remembrancer, in a letter wherein he also said that he "always" knew in his heart Walt Whitman's mind to be more like his own than any other living man's. [7]

Awareness of Whitman's poetry was consciously in Hopkins' mind by 1874, if not indeed earlier, for when he reported to Bridges in 1882 that he had read some half-dozen poems by Whitman, he mentioned the fact that he had read Saintsbury's laudatory review of *Leaves of Grass*, including some quotations from Whitman, in the *Academy* of October 10, 1874. [8] Precisely what Hopkins wrote as a list of his Whitman reading is as follows:

... (1) 'Pete' ["Come Up from the Fields Father"] in the library at Bedford Square (and perhaps something else; if so I forget), which you pointed out; (2) two pieces in the *Athenaeum* or *Academy,* one of the Man-of-War Bird, the other beginning 'Spirit that formed this scene'; (3) short extracts in a review by Saintsbury in the *Academy* [of *Leaves of Grass*: Oct. 10, 1874, pp. 398-400]; this is all I remember. I cannot have read more than half a dozen pieces at most. [9]

But this is not a clear, nor a clearly all-inclusive, list of what he had read of Whitman's.

When, in 1882, Bridges had read in manuscript Hopkins' "The Leaden Echo" and "The Golden Echo" he wrote to Hopkins and suggested that these poems showed the influence of Whitman. Hopkins replied vehemently with a letter of great length; and he followed this with another letter three days later in which he called the first letter his "de-Whitmaniser" and showed that he was conscious of its vehemence by saying further, "I believe it was stern and a bit of a mouther." [10] Moreover, years before this and years afterward he revealed his vivid awareness of

Whitman. Earlier, in a letter to Bridges in January, 1879, he sent the remark that "even Walt Whitman nurses the sick." Later in April, 1884, he wrote to Bridges from Dublin and mentioned that he had recently read samples of the poetry of Sidney Lanier, and thought them "something like E. A. Poe, something like Whitman." [11]

Eleanor Ruggles has already been quoted as declaring the question of Whitman's influence upon Hopkins "unsolved." Yet she ponders over it for more than three pages, [12] and calls the statement by Hopkins concerning the similarity of Whitman's mind and his own a "remarkable and mysterious" confession, remarkable because of its degree of truth, and mysterious because "we can never be quite sure which ones among these several likenesses Hopkins himself had apprehended"—and then suggests some five likenesses. Indicating parallelisms she says, first, that two lines, "which Hopkins had not read," and which tell of Whitman's watch beside a dying soldier boy, have their paraphrase in a line of Hopkins' "Felix Randal." But it is not at all sure that Hopkins had not read the two lines by Whitman. She quotes them without stating source:

> One turns to me his appealing eyes—poor boy! I never
>   knew you,
> Yet I think I could not refuse this moment to die for
>   you, if that would save you.

I find, however, that they stand in "The Dresser," a poem first printed in 1865, in *Drum-Taps*. [13] The 1876 "Author's Edition" of *Leaves of Grass* (Camden, New Jersey) includes the *Drum-Taps* poems. Another poem in *Drum-Taps,* appearing only a few pages away from "The Dresser," is "Come Up from the Fields Father," the "Pete" poem that Hopkins said he had read in the library in Bridges' home at 52 Bedford Square, London. This poem of Whitman's experience in nursing the sick and wounded may certainly have been the "something else" that Hopkins "perhaps" had read there. Hopkins may have seen this, along with the "Pete" poem, in late July, 1877, when he seems to have made an overnight visit at Bridges'; he wrote on July 23, 1877, to Bridges, that he looked forward to "seeing and hearing your treasures (poetical and musical)." [14] When in 1879 he wrote to Bridges that "even Walt Whitman nurses the sick," he used a casual tone as if assuming that Bridges knew this too, as if he and Bridges might together have read "The Dresser" or have spoken of it. [15] "Felix Randal" was written by April 28, 1880. [16]

Hopkins' statement that Bridges had pointed out poetry by Whitman, in his own library, to Hopkins, indicates further knowledge by Hopkins of Whitman: for clearly Bridges had talked to Hopkins of this American poet's work, some of which he had in his own library. He could scarcely have failed to mention the long poem containing the "handkerchief of the Lord," "stallion," "spotted hawk swoops by," "seas of bright juice," "Failing to find me at first, keep encouraged," and "drift it in lacy jags" passages—whether that poem, now known as "Song of Myself," was untitled as in the 1855 edition, or given a title: it was headed "Walt Whitman" in the New York edition of 1867 and in the Camden edition of 1876. These passages are discussed in this article.

Miss Ruggles says, furthermore, that there is what she calls one hint of direct influence of Whitman in Hopkins' poetry. She points out that in *Democratic Vistas* Whitman presents Christ as "with bent head, brooding love and peace, like a dove"; and that Hopkins, in "God's Grandeur," has "what seems to be a shadow, a reflection of Whitman's image as he describes the Holy Ghost, the Comforter in form of a dove who

over the bent
World broods with warm breast and with ah! bright wings."

She declares that Hopkins "had never read *Democratic Vistas*," but that somewhere he may have seen or heard Whitman's phrase quoted, and that possibly the thoughts of the two poets seized independently on the same words. Again, however, we must say that it is not at all sure that Hopkins "had never read" something of Whitman's, for *Democratic Vistas* was included in the two-volume "Author's Edition" of 1876. In the second volume, *Two Rivulets*, etc., on page 52 of *Democratic Vistas*, appears the phrase in question. As we have seen, the first volume has the "Pete" poem that Hopkins remembered reading. [17]

F. O. Matthiessen, in his *American Renaissance*, has a discussion of Whitman and Hopkins that Charney properly enough ranks high as "quite acute on the style and characterization of the two." [18] He suggests direct influence when he says that "To the Man-of-War Bird" is "similar enough for Hopkins to have possibly received the hint for his theme [in "The Windhover"] from it." He quotes the first four lines of Hopkins' poem and the last five lines of Whitman's and says that the "eagle's muscles are flaccid by contrast" to the windhover's, and that the difference between the movement of Hopkins' bird and that of Whitman's is "overwhelming." He points out, too, the similarity to Whitman in Hopkins' Poem 61 that I had observed independently and indicate farther on in this article. [19]

Various other scholars and critics of Hopkins, generally speaking, if they mention Whitman, either brush aside the suggestion of influence or do little more than allow the broad possibility of it. Peters in 1948 states that Hopkins has been "mentioned in one breath with Walt Whitman"; but Peters decides against the implication of influence, and declares flatly that "Bridges first launched this comparison, but Hopkins repudiated it." [20] Heywood seems definitely to oppose the idea of any specific influence from Whitman as he asserts:

While admitting a certain resemblance between their styles . . . he [Hopkins] concludes it is a case of extremes meeting: 'This savagery of his art, this rhythm in its last ruggedness and decomposition into common prose, comes near the last elaboration of mine.' [21]

Writing of Hopkins as reader and critic, Gardner says that Hopkins "deliberately avoided" "the insidious attraction of Whitman." [22]

Yet what surely might have been said is rather that Hopkins had stated in a letter that he intended in the future to avoid reading Whitman. For we find that the pertinent evidence, written to Bridges in 1882, stands as follows:

> ... I may as well say what I should not otherwise have said, that I always knew in my heart Walt Whitman's mind to be more like my own than any other man's living. As he is a very great scoundrel this is not a pleasant confession. And this also makes me the more desirous to read him and the more determined that I will not. .... [23]

Moreover, the same letter had commenced with an account of what Hopkins had indeed previously read of Whitman's poetry (and hence could not avoid knowing about), and the letter had dwelt in considerable detail upon the rhythmic qualities of Whitman, and thus showed that Hopkins had already been deeply impressed by his knowledge of Whitman. Hopkins reveals a remarkably good recollection of the Whitman poetry that he had read: although he slightly misquotes a line from one poem, he does this from memory, and does it a considerable time—possibly several years—after reading, and he seems to remember well the context wherein the passage occurs; furthermore, he refers in the same letter specifically and with good memory to another poem by Whitman, read possibly several years before.

Gardner also asserts that "at considerable length, Hopkins repudiates the suggestion of imitation" after Bridges has accused him of "being unduly influenced by the free rhythms of Walt Whitman." Yet Gardner, with his usual care and thoroughness, continues to consider the accusation, and soon announces:

> ... Hopkins was right in giving Greek choric metre priority as the prototype of The Echoes; but there was also much

probability in the suggestion made by Bridges, that the immediate stimulus provided by Whitman's original contribution to English rhythm was greater than Hopkins himself had suspected. [24]

In a different connection, and several chapters farther along, Gardner volunteers the observation that "In the closing quintet of *Pied Beauty* there is a capacious Whitman-like acceptance of *natural* pieings and perversities, a flux of Heraclitean opposites which culminates in praise for the super-Heraclitean God." [25] Gardner in still another chapter says that *"Leaves of Grass* opens with transports which are quite Hopkinsian"—and here he quotes not from the long opening poem of 1855 that was to be entitled "Walt Whitman" and "Song of Myself," nor from "Inscription" that opens the 1867 edition, but rather from the brief, later-inserted "One's Self I Sing" that opens the 1876 and later editions that I have consulted. [26]

And as we look for ourselves at the letter that Hopkins called his "de-Whitmaniser" we come, it seems to me, to the conclusions (1) that perhaps he doth protest too much against Bridges' imputation, and (2) that he leaves the door open for the possibility of Whitman's having influenced his diction. We remember that he himself referred to the letter as "a bit of a mouther"; and we find the letter ending with this one-sentence paragraph: "I wish I had not spent so much time defending the piece." Indicating what he has read by Whitman, he says, "I cannot have read more than half a dozen pieces at most." But in the next paragraph he conscientiously declares that what he has read may suffice to constitute a definite stimulus or even an influence:

This, though very little, is quite enough to give a strong impression of his [Whitman's] marked and original manner and way of thought and in particular of his rhythm. It might be even enough, I shall not deny, to originate or, much more, influence another's style.

After a long defense of "The Leaden Echo" and "The Golden Echo" from the charge of imitating the rhythm of Whitman, he turns to the question of word choice, and says frankly:

About diction the matter does not allow me so clearly to point out my independence as about rhythm. I cannot think that the present piece owes anything to him. I hope not, here especially, for it is not even spoken in my own person but in that of St. Winefred's maidens. . . . [27]

This is obvious indication that what he had read by Whitman he had read with analytic thoughtfulness, that Whitman's diction had made a consciously strong appeal to Hopkins, and that he felt fairly sure that in some of his poems there could be found words that echoed the diction of the American. [28]

II

In 1935 Charles Madge pointed out impressively the use by Hopkins of certain words that Whitman had employed. [29] Since his article will usually be difficult to consult, I briefly indicate here some of his pertinent findings. Whitman had written in the first poem of *Leaves of Grass* (the poem later called "Walt Whitman" or "Song of Myself"):

I depart as air . . . I shake my white locks at the runaway
sun,
I effuse my flesh in eddies and drift it in lacy jags. [30]

Madge insists that Hopkins, like Whitman, shows "violent self-identification with kinaesthetic Nature, and the exalted physical states of emphatic hyperaesthesia"—that Hopkins, like Whitman, is an "exponent of *lacy jags*." Madge finds in the Englishman's poem "A Vision of the Mermaids" (written in 1862) diction that indicates echoes of Whitman in the early writing by Hopkins: "lace of rosy weed," "fretted falls," "flesh-flowers," "dainty-delicate fretted fringe of fingers." He points out that in the intermediate period Hopkins uses such phrases as "the midriff . . . laced with fire of stress," "youth fretted in a bloomfall," "lace . . . footfretted," "How lovely the elder brother's Life all laced in the other's Love-laced!" And in Hopkins' later poetry Madge finds emphasis upon the *laciness* of nature: "See banks and brake Now leavèd how thick! lacèd they are again With fretty chervil, look. . . ."

Madge shows, furthermore, that Hopkins feels nature to be "naturally juicy and ripe"; he quotes (from the 1877 sonnet "Spring"):

> The glassy peartree leaves and blooms, they brush
> The descending blue; that blue is all in a rush
> With richness; the racing lambs too have fair their fling.
> What is all the juice and all this joy?

And he calls attention again to Whitman, who had written:

> Hefts of the moving world, at innocent gambols, silently
> rising, freshly exuding,
> Scooting obliquely high and low.
> Something I cannot see puts upward libidinous prongs;
> Seas of bright juice suffuse heaven.

Later Hopkins wrote, in Poem 104:

> Or like a juicy and jostling shock
> Of bluebells sheaved in May
> Or wind-long fleeces on the flock
> A day off shearing day.

I give no more of Madge—but this is enough to show that he provides impressive evidence that Whitman's words did at times reappear in Hopkins' work.

III

I interpose here an account of a striking similarity that I observe to exist in rhythmic and alliterative technique between Whitman and Hopkins (e.g., in "The Leaden

Echo"). The ninth line from the end of Whitman's poem referred to in Section II above is the one containing the "lacy jags" phrase treated by Madge. Two lines below it we find this passage, occupying the emphatic final position in the poem (I italicize the impressively alliterating letters):

You will *h*ardly know *w*ho I am, or *w*hat I mean;
But I shall be good *h*ealth to you nevertheless,
And *f*ilter and *f*ibre your blood.
*F*ailing to *f*etch me at *f*irst, *k*eep encouraged;
*M*issing *m*e one pla*c*e, *s*earch another;
I *st*op *s*ome *wh*ere, *w*aiting for you.

Remembering the alliterative intricacy of "The Leaden Echo," we need not wonder on the basis of even these Whitman lines alone that Bridges surmised the influence of the American.

IV

Some time ago, before I had any knowledge of Madge's observations, several noteworthy parallels in diction and ideas in the work of Whitman and Hopkins struck my attention as indicating definite echoes of Whitman by Hopkins. Here are specific instances, in this section.

Instance 1. Whitman commences the poem now called "Song of Myself" with the self-centered.

I celebrate myself,

and then proceeds by ranging in vigorous enumeration over a great number of types of people, of both sexes, of varying ages and races and widely varying occupations and conditions, and he interjects:

And these one and all tend inward to me, and I
tend outward to them;
And such as it is to be of these, more or less, I am.

Also:

> I am the mate and companion of people, all just as
> immortal and fathomless as myself;
> (They do not know how immortal, but I know.)

Hopkins wrote, in Poem 72:

> I am all at once what Christ is, since he was what I am, and
> This Jack, joke, poor potsherd, patch, matchwood, immortal
> diamond,
> Is immortal diamond.

Instance 2. Referring with love to numerous animals and birds as being superior to man, Whitman remarks that they do not worship externals:

> Not one kneels to another, nor to his kind that lived
> thousands of years ago. . . .

Hopkins presents in Poem 61 this emphasis upon the greatness of self and the value of independence in "self"-ness:

> To man, that needs would worship block or barren stone,
> Our law says: Love what are love's worthiest, were
> all known;
> World's loveliest—men's selves. Self flashes off
> frame and face.
> What do then? how meet beauty? Merely meet it, own
> Home at heart, heaven's sweet gift. . . .

Similar concern for the self appears in Poem 71:

> Soul, self; come, poor Jackself, I do advise
> You, jaded, let be; call off thoughts awhile
> Elsewhere. . . .

Instance 3. Near the memorable end of Whitman's poem come these lines, stressing God in self and God in mankind, to be seen in faces:

I hear and behold God in every object, yet understand
  God not in the least,
Nor do I understand who there can be more wonderful
  than myself.
Why should I wish to see God better than this day?
I see something of God each hour of the twenty-four
  and each moment then;
In the faces of men and women I see God, and in
  my own face in the glass. . . .

Hopkins' Poem 57 gives notably similar emphasis upon
self and upon God or Christ in one's self and visible in
the faces of others:

As kingfishers catch fire, dragonflies dráw fláme;
As tumbled over rim in roundy wells
Stones ring; like each tucked string tells, each hung bell's
Bow swung finds tongue to fling out broad its name;
Each mortal thing does one thing and the same:
Deals out that being indoors each one dwells;
Selves—goes itself; *myself* it speaks and spells,
Crying *Whát I dó is me*: *for that I came.*
I say móre: the just man justices;
Keèps gráce: thát keeps all his goings graces;
Acts in God's eye what in God's eye he is—
Christ—for Christ plays in ten thousand places,
Lovely in limbs, and lovely in eyes not his
To the Father through the features of men's faces.

Instance 4. Bridges pointed out as a fault of taste in Hopkins "the affectation in metaphor . . . where the hills are
'as a stallion stalwart, very-violet-sweet,'"[31] and so directed more than ordinary attention by readers to that
startling passage in "Hurrahing in Harvest" (1877). A
stimulus may have come from Whitman. Not many lines
after the "scented gift and remembrancer" passage that
Hopkins recollected so well, Whitman had presented a
memorable line:

And the look of the bay mare shames silliness out of me.

Then somewhat farther along (Section 32) he had written:

> A gigantic beauty of a stallion, fresh and responsive
>   to my caresses,
> Head high in the forehead, wide between the ears,
> Limbs glossy and supple, tail dusting the ground,
> .   .   .   .
> I but use you a moment, then I resign you, stallion;
> .   .   .   .
> I skirt the sierras. . . .

Instance 5. Only a few lines above the "lacy jags" line, Whitman had presented this:

> The spotted hawk swoops by and accuses me—he complains
>   of my gab and my loitering.
> I too am not a bit tamed—I too am untranslatable;
> I sound my barbaric yawp over the roofs of the world.

Hopkins may have meditated upon the symbol of the hawk as representing physical beauty and joy in physical, fiery vigor (he calls the symbol "windhover" rather than "hawk") and reacted differently from Whitman: his windhover, like Whitman's hawk, swooped, and it glided, and had brute beauty and valour, pride and plume. But the windhover inspired no companion, untamed attitude in Hopkins—his heart (relatively "in hiding" as compared to the hawk or windhover soaring over the roofs of the world) he had disciplined to a plodding, lowly life of self-sacrifice inspired by Christ his Lord; his natural fire he had voluntarily reduced to embers; and he was not sorry, for he felt, seemed to see, the shining glory of the sheer plod of his devotion, the gold-vermilion glow of inner satisfaction at his pious restraint of his blazing enthusiasm over physical beauty and his flaming joy in physical beauty that had excited and sustained, and would, if permitted, even yet excite and sustain for him a sense of mere worldly pleasure. [32]

Instance 6. Bridges indicated that "The Windhover: To Christ Our Lord" had been written by May 30, 1877. He also indicated that "Hurrahing in Harvest" (already referred to for its "stallion" figure of speech) had been written by September 1, of the same year. [33] The latter poem commences: "Summer ends now; now, barbarous in beauty, the stooks arise." I put it within the realm of probability that Whitman's use of "barbaric" with a startling, because highly favorable connotation ("I sound my barbaric yawp over the roofs of the world"), that Whitman's use, I say, had lingered, perhaps unconsciously, in the mind of Hopkins, and led him to the choice of "barbarous" in the glorious and famous description of the stooks as "barbarous in beauty."

Instance 7. "The Habit of Perfection" is printed by Bridges as one of Hopkins' "Early Poems"; and we are told that there are two autograph versions, the earlier dated "January 18, 19, 1866." [34] In this superbly polished little poem Hopkins states his wish to have none of the physical pleasures of any of the sense organs; he insists that he will have richness of the spirit only when he is clothed in poverty with reference to the things of the material world. Sounds heard, the production of sounds as speech, sights, taste, fragrance, touch by hands and by feet; *all these delights, in a stanza for each, are caused to suggest the greater pleasures of the spiritual existence with God in Heaven or of the ascetic way of living in this world* when material pleasures of the senses have been renounced.

Now the "Walt Whitman" (later "Song of Myself") poem in *Leaves of Grass*—it is the untitled first poem in the 1855 edition—is a wordy development of the theme that *through all the senses a person is made aware of the glory of life and of God,* and of the mystery of God which brings no fear with it. Near the end (a few lines before the passage, noted above in connection with "The Windhover," that tells of the spotted hawk swooping by) Whitman declares:

> (No array of terms san say how much I am at peace
> about God, and about death.)

76

> I hear and behold God in every object, yet understand
> > God not in the least,
> Nor do I understand who there can be more wonderful
> > than myself.

At the beginning of the poem he states this theme in somewhat greater detail: see lines 6-29, wherein he cites pleasures of fragrance, taste, touch, sounds, speaking, "a few embraces," "the play of shine and shade on the trees as the supple boughs wag," "the delight along, or in the rush of the streets," and "the feeling of health"; and declares that "You shall possess the good of the earth and sun" if you visit him, ending with these lines (indicating notably intentional variety of activities of the senses):

> You shall not look through my eyes either, nor take
> > things from me:
> You shall listen to all sides, and filter them from
> > yourself.

This theme is developed, in Whitman's own way, in the body of the poem. Such lines as these—and there are many others—remind us of what is being developed, namely, a joy in the use of *all* the senses, and an awareness that the material world, through sensation, leads to communion with God:

(1) Clear and sweet is my Soul, and clear and sweet
       is all that is not my Soul.

(2) Welcome is every organ and attribute of me, and
       of any man hearty and clean.

(3) The press of my foot to the earth springs a hundred
       affections.

(4) Seeing, hearing, feeling, are miracles, and each
       part and tag of me is a miracle.

(5) The air tastes good to my palate.

(6) With the twirl of my tongue I encompass worlds,
       and volumes of worlds.

(7) I think I will do nothing now but listen.

(8) I merely stir, press, feel with my fingers, and
       am happy;
   To touch my person to some one else's is about
       as much as I can stand.

(9) At the cider-mill, tasting the sweets of the brown
　　　　　　mash, sucking the juice through a straw.
(10) 　　　　　I accept reality, and dare not question it;
　　　　Materialism first and last imbuing.
　　　　Hurrah for positive science! ...
　　　　Gentlemen [scientists]! to you the first honors
　　　　　　always:
　　　　Your facts are useful and real—and yet they are
　　　　　　not my dwelling;
　　　　(I but enter by them to an area of my dwelling.) ... ²⁵

Thus when we read this poem by Whitman and then read
Hopkins' "The Habit of Perfection" we may plausibly
sense a close relationship: they have the same theme.
　At one point Whitman declares:

　　I know perfectly well my own egotism;
　I know my omnivorous lines, and will not write any less;
　And would fetch you, whoever you are, flush with myself.

　　　No words of routine are mine,
　But abruptly to question, to leap beyond, yet nearer bring.

These lines offer strong challenge to a person possessed
of such an attitude toward poetic composition as Hopkins
had—an attitude of using fewer words, and using polished words of compact, unquestioning assurance. We
muse, moreover, when we find, a little farther on, Whitman presenting this line:

　　He most honors my style who learns under it to
　　　　　destroy the teacher.

Hopkins may in his poem be making a brief, succinct,
and polished parallel to Whitman's challenging song of
himself, even though the Englishman makes no outright
reference to the American. "The Habit of Perfection" is
a development of Whitman's theme in Hopkins' style.

V

As for Whitman's mind being more like Hopkins' own
than any other man's living, Philip Henderson in his book

The Poet and Society has made an interesting attempt to sum up the situation:

. . . . Whitman represented all that side of himself which he [Hopkins] had vainly tried to suppress in the name of religion; he found in Whitman that same overmastering virile energy and turbulence, that luxuriant sensuality, that devouring love of the physical beauty of men and the world. . . . [36]

I object to the implication that the English poet had tried to suppress *all* the Whitman side in himself. Hopkins called Whitman "scoundrel" only in the sense that he also in his correspondence [37] called Goethe "scoundrel"— Whitman seemed to him socially, morally, and religiously unbridled, crude, and flauntingly so. He strove, and continued to strive, even as did Whitman for the joy in and exercise of and devotion to originality in artistic creation; he too sang a song of himself; he too sang of the "dearest freshness deep down things" as he only himself had perceived, and had found words for, things and their attributes. He, however, put upon himself—not upon things and other persons, but, consciously, upon himself — the restraint and constraint of observing religious and social morality and of spiritual subservience to Christ his Lord, to God, or to Mary, the Virgin Mother, "the Rose in a Mystery"; he would not allow himself to take a hawk-like joy in the beauty of this world. Finally, he put upon himself, again possibly in conscious difference from Whitman, the restraint and constraint of very great musical polish—he had studied Whitman, had admired, and had determined to do otherwise—; he, in his own artistic manner, would endeavor to have no Whitmanesque "savagery" of art, no "rhythm in its last ruggedness and decomposition into common prose"; he would provide palpably intended ornamentation and conscious control for artistic beauty. He once wrote Bridges that "one ought to be independent but not unimpressionable: that wd. be to refuse education." And at another time he asserted:

... every true poet, I thought, must be original and originality a condition of poetic genius; so that each poet is like a species in nature (*not* an *individuum genericum* or *specificum*) and can never recur. That nothing shd. be old or borrowed however cannot be. . . . [38]

This article, then, has presented evidence of actual and of possible influence by Whitman upon Hopkins. Though it is not yet certain exactly how much of Whitman's poetry Hopkins was closely aware of, he clearly had read some of Whitman, and that with seriousness, careful analysis, and subsequent frank avowal of possible influence. Echoes of Whitman, or apparent echoes, have been cited. At the very least, echoes and parallels of Whitman in the poetry of Hopkins, when recognized as such, may be said to illuminate understanding and increase appreciation of the work of both poets—especially of Hopkins.

NOTES

1 Eleanor Ruggles, *Gerard Manley Hopkins: A Life* (New York: Norton, 1944), p. 221.

2 Terence Heywood, "Gerard Manley Hopkins: His Literary Ancestry," *English,* III (1940, pp. 16-24; reprinted from *Poetry,* LIV (1939), pp. 209-18, 271-79.

3 Claude Colleer Abbott (ed.), *Further Letters of Gerard Manley Hopkins including his Correspondence with Coventry Patmore* (London: Oxford University Press, 1938), p. 62. Hereinafter this book is referred to as *"Further Letters."*

4 *Ibid.,* p. 62n.

5 W. H. Gardner (ed.), *Poems of Gerard Manley Hopkins* (3rd. ed.; London: Oxford University Press, 1948), p. 248. This book is hereinafter referred to as *"Poems, 3rd. ed."* Quotations from Hopkins' poetry, unless otherwise stated, are from this book. The passage quoted above, from a letter to Bridges, suggests rather clearly that Hopkins knew that Bridges had in his personal library a copy of Whitman's works—possibly the 2-vol. "Author's Edition" of 1876. See below, in the discussion of a remark by Eleanor Ruggles.

6 This and other quotations from Whitman's poetry, except as otherwise stated, are from the 1867 ed. (New York) of

Leaves of Grass; the version of them in the Author's Edition (Camden, New Jersey, 1876) is the same; the 1855 version of the passage quoted—see the Facsimile Edition (New York, 1939)—differs very slightly, usually only in a little punctuation or spelling.

7 Claude Colleer Abbott (ed.), *The Letters of Gerard Manley Hopkins to Robert Bridges* (London: Oxford University Press, 1935), p. 155. This book is hereinafter referred to as *"Letters, I."*

8 W. H. Gardner declares that 1874 was "an intensely formative year in the development of Hopkins' theories on poetic rhythm and diction." See his *Gerard Manley Hopkins (1844-1889): A Study of Poetic Idiosyncrasy in Relation to Poetic Tradition,* II (London: Secker & Warburg, 1949), p. 108. Hereinafter this book is referred to as "Gardner, II."

9 *Letters,* I, p. 154.

10 See *Ibid.,* pp. 153-58.

11 *Ibid.,* pp. 63, 192.

12 Ruggles, pp. 221-25.

13 *Walt Whitman's Drum-Taps* (New York, 1865), p. 32.

14 *Letters,* I, pp. 41-42. He may have read Whitman in Bridges' library at some time, or at some other time also: e.g., August, 1878—see *Letters,* I, pp. 57-58. One should remember that Hopkins, through Bridges or another, may have known something of Whitman's work much earlier. See footnote 28, below.

15 See *Ibid.,* p. 63.

16 *Poems,* 3rd. ed., p. 237.

17 *Democratic Vistas* had been published separately (Washington, D.C., 1871), and the phrase is on p. 52 of this also.

18 For Charney, see footnote 32, below.

19 F. O. Matthiessen, *American Renaissance* (Cambridge, Mass.: Harvard University Press, 1941), pp. 584-92.

20 W. A. M. Peters, S.J., *Gerard Manley Hopkins: A Critical Essay towards the Understanding of his Poetry* (London: Oxford University Press, 1948), pp. xvii, 173.

21 See footnote 2, above.

22 Gardner, II, p. 195n.

23 *Letters,* I, p. 155.

24 Gardner, II, pp. 105-08. One critic has presented and scanned three lines by Whitman as written in Sprung Rhythm, paralleling Hopkins' work in "The Wreck of the *Deutschland*"; but he has done this in a footnote, and has ventured to make no comment. See K. R. Srinivasa Iyengar, *Gerard Manley Hopkins . . .* (London: Oxford University Press, 1948), p. 160.

25 *Ibid.*, p. 250. It is worth noting that "Pied Beauty" is chronologically placed by Bridges between "The Windhover" and "Hurrahing in Harvest," two other poems that are suggested in this article as showing possible Whitman influence. See *Poems*, 3rd. ed., pp. 228-29.

26 Gardner, II, p. 335.

27 *Letters*, I, p. 158.

28 A note here may be allowed to show that others in England had read Whitman before 1864. Sir Charles Tennyson states (*Alfred Tennyson* [New York, 1949], p. 307) that *Leaves of Grass* was among the books that Alfred read aloud to his wife (according to her diary) in the winter of 1857-58. We know that other Englishmen besides Tennyson were early readers of Whitman; and Hopkins as a schoolboy in the late 'fifties and early 'sixties was writing poetry and of course reading and talking of poetry. He might have been aware then of *Leaves of Grass*, which Tennyson read "by way of curiosity." Copies of it were being sold by a book-peddler in England before one came, in December, 1856, to W. M. Rosetti's hands. D. G. Rosetti referred to it in a letter in April, 1856, to William Allingham as having been written by "that Orson of yours." W. M. Rosetti was to call its author "the real American poet," and "a man enormously greater than Longfellow." Charles Kingsley disapproved of its author because he was coarse and sensual. The British *Saturday Review*, on March 15, 1856, had denounced it strongly: "If the *Leaves of Grass* should come into anybody's possession, our advice is to throw them instantly behind the fire"—such a remark might arouse undergraduate curiosity at any time. Harold Blodgett, who points out these items, also says, indeed, that "John Addington Symonds and other university young men had been reading the 1860 edition of the *Leaves* in their Oxford rooms"; and that Symonds found his friend Myers reading Whitman at Cambridge in 1865. (See *Walt Whitman in England* [Cornell University Press, 1934], pp. 7-20, 59.) So Hopkins might even have listened to someone else read aloud from *Leaves of Grass* in early impressionable days, and thus have been well aware of at least the long first poem, even though he might years later write to Bridges and indicate in strict truth that what he had read with his own eyes had been very little. In August, 1864, he plumed himself (see *Further Letters*, p. 67) on having met Christina Rosetti and other literary people at the Gurneys'.

29 "What Is All This Juice?—Hopkins and the Victorian Conception of Nature," *New Verse*, No. 14 (April, 1935), pp. 17-21.

30 The version printed in 1867 and 1876 differs from this only in the use of a dash for the four dots, a semicolon for the comma after "sun," and a comma inserted after "eddies."

31 *Poems*, 3rd ed., p. 204.

32 Raymond V. Schoder includes useful summaries and criticisms of a number of the better-known, varying interpretations of "The Windhover" as introduction to his own lengthy interpretation, in "What Does *The Windhover* Mean?"—see pp. 275-306 of *Immortal Diamond: Studies in Gerard Manley Hopkins,* ed. Norman Weyand (New York, 1949). See also F. N. Lees' exposition, "The Windhover," in *Scrutiny,* XVII (1950), pp. 32-37, and the eclectic critical summary by Maurice Charney on pp. 309-10 of his excellent "A Bibliographical Study of Hopkins Criticism, 1918-1949," *Thought,* XXV (1950), pp. 297-326. In "Hopkins' 'The Windhover': A New Simplification," *Modern Language Notes,* LXVI (1951), pp. 366-70, Frederick L. Gwynn is interesting, but I prefer my interpretation: I do not think that "the *whole* poem is about a bird," any more than the *whole* of "The Caged Skylark," or "Spring," or "The Starlight Night" is about the thing named in the title.

My own interpretation of "The Windhover," given in the paragraph to which this footnote is attached, may be of especial interest to some readers, because of the great popularity of this poem, and also because of dissatisfaction accorded to one or another of the previous interpretations.

33 *Poems*, 3rd. ed., pp. 228-229. Hopkins, however, revised "the Falcon sonnet" later, slightly—see *Letters,* I, p. 56 (July 16, 1878) and p. 85 (June 22, 1879).

34 *Ibid.*, p. 217.

35 These ten passages appear in the following sections of "Walt Whitman" in the 1867 and 1876 editions of *Leaves of Grass*: 3, 3, 14, 24, 24, 25, 26, 27, 33, 33. They appear with slight difference, chiefly in punctuation, in the 1855 version, which has no title or section numbering.

36 "Gerard Manley Hopkins" in Philip Henderson, *The Poet and Society* (London, 1939), pp. 103-31.

37 Claude Colleer Abbott (ed.), *The Correspondence of Gerard Manley Hopkins and Richard Watson Dixon* (London: Oxford University Press, 1935), p. 25. Here Hopkins puts Burns in the same class.

38 *Letters,* I. p. 80; *Further Letters,* p. 222 (to Patmore, Oct. 6, 1886).

Margaret R. Stobie

PATMORE'S THEORY AND HOPKINS' PRACTICE

It is remarkable that often the near past is the most obscure period of history. This hooded quality of the prox-
imate is exemplified in the fate of the prosody of Hopkins. Bridges, publishing Hopkins' poems thirty years
after his death, comments: "It was an idiosyncrasy of
this student's mind to push everything to its logical extreme, and take pleasure in a paradoxical result; as may
be seen in his prosody where a simple theory seems to
be used only as a basis for unexampled liberty." Taken
up with later theories which were engaging the interests of
poets in 1918, Bridges did not bother to mention what
the "simple theory" was, although by his tone he must
have been familiar with it. It was left for Mr. Harold
Whitehall, in 1944, to discover that this theory was the
so-called dipodic theory which had first been announced
by Patmore. Mr. Whitehall says:

Hopkins' sprung rhythm, and for that matter most of his running rhythm, follows Patmore's theories almost to the letter.
Yet Patmore and Hopkins never saw how they complemented
each other. Although Hopkins had undoubtedly read the Patmore essay by 1881 . . . he was too limited by conventional
metrical theory and by concessions to stanzaic form to realize
its bearing on the explanation of his own work. Patmore, for
his part, . . . was puzzled by the appearance of the poems in
Hopkins' manuscript . . . and was misled by the abrupt juxtapo-
sition of stresses which is Hopkins' chief metrical innovation.
If accident of time and friendship had permitted an early meeting between the two men—the virtuosic dipodic practitioner
and our first dipodic theorist—Hopkins' poems might have
yielded metrical secrets in his own lifetime. [1]

The close relationship between the metrical theories of
Patmore and of Hopkins, which Mr. Whitehall notes here,

is indeed so remarkable that it is almost incredible that Hopkins was not familiar with Patmore's "Essay on English Metrical Law" until so late a date. Such ignorance of it is the more unlikely in view of the great contemporary interest which the essay aroused. It was first published in 1856, and in a note to the 1886 reprinting of it Patmore comments upon its intervening popularity and influence: "I have seen with pleasure that, since then, its main principles have been quietly adopted by most writers on the subject in periodicals and elsewhere." Nor is Patmore flattering himself, for poets and prosodians alike, apart from their interest in the dipodic theory as such, found in the essay the first intelligent attempt to solve a problem which interested them all—how to include within the principles of English versification the peculiarities of the newly recovered body of Old English poetry. In particular, Patmore's theory was of great interest to the Oxford set with whom he was on familiar terms when the essay was first published and which included not only Burne-Jones and William Morris, but also R. W. Dixon, who took his degree in that year and who was shortly to become Hopkins' schoolmaster. So, even if it could be demonstrably proved that Hopkins did not read the essay until about 1880, it would still be most unlikely that he should not be familiar with its theories, which were a topic of general discussion. It would seem, on the contrary, to be strongly probable that Hopkins became acquainted with the theory either through Dixon, or before he left Oxford in 1867, eleven years after the essay was published, or during his seven years of poetic silence. Such a conjecture gains some measure of support from Bridges' comment, in which he suggests Hopkins' early familiarity with the "simple theory," and from Hopkins' note on "The Wreck of the Deutschland": "I had long had haunting my ear the echo of a new rhythm which now I realised on paper. . . . I do not say the idea is altogether new . . . but no one has professedly used it and made it the principle throughout, that I know of." [2]

Certainly, the "Author's Preface" which Hopkins wrote in 1883 sounds like a summary of Patmore, in its remarks on common English rhythm, on rising and falling stress, on reversed or counterpointed feet, on run-on scansion, on anacrusis, metrical pauses, and so forth. On the other hand, Hopkins makes some important corrections and additions to Patmore's theory, both in the Preface and in the body of his poems, which subsequent dipodists either have not understood or have ignored. These corrections in themselves are valuable enough to merit a re-examination of Patmore, but in turn they throw some light on those problems which Mr. Whitehall, in his excellent article, feels are still obscure. The most important of these problems concern the meaning of Hopkins' term "sprung" rhythm, his manipulating of secondary stress, and his preoccupation with stanza forms.

II

The terms of the "law" which Patmore abruptly announces are as interesting for their arbitrariness as they are for their implications. They are important enough to quote at some length:

Nothing but the unaccountable disregard, by prosodians, of final pauses could have prevented the observation of the great general law, which I believe that I am now, for the first time, stating, that *the elementary measure, or integer, of English verse is double the measure of Ordinary prose,*—that is to say, it is the space which is bounded by *alternate* accents; *that every verse proper contains two, three or four of these 'metres,'* or, as with a little allowance they may be called, '*dipodes*'; *and that there is properly no such thing as hypercatalexis.* All English verses in common cadence are therefore dimeters, trimeters, or tetrameters, and consist, when they are *full,* i.e., without *catalexis,* of eight, twelve, or sixteen syllables. Verses in triple cadence obey the same law, only their length never . . . exceeds that of the trimeter, on account of the great number of syllables or places of syllables (twenty-four) which would be involved in a tetrameter in such cadence. Monometers cannot stand in series as verse though . . . the effect of their introduction is often admirable. [3]

In the first italicized section of this law, there are two arbitrary assumptions. The first is that the normal measure of prose is of either two or three syllables: that is, prose measures conform to the descriptive terms of iambic, trochaic, anapaestic, or dactylic feet. Patmore gives no reason for this assumption, and indeed, as we shall see from his own prose, it is unsupportable. The second, equally arbitrary assumption is that poetic measure is twice that of prose. It contains *two* iambic, trochaic, etc. feet, and may therefore be described as dipodic.

The first deduction based on these assumptions is in the second italicized section, "that every verse proper contains two, three, or four of these 'metres'." This deduction is not more reliable than its bases, but it is important to Patmore's system of scansion. If a verse is not full, it is completed of necessity in one of several ways. Either the time of the missing syllables is made up by a pause at the end of the line as in these dipodic dimeters:

One road leads to Lóndon,   (pause of two syllables)
One road leads to Wáles;   (pause of three syllables)

or the measure is completed in the unemphatic syllables at the beginning of the next line:

> Mérrily did we dróp
> Below the kírk, below the híll
> Below the líght-house tóp;

or individual syllables within the line may be so weighted as to receive the time of two or more syllables, as in the line

> Cóme, sée rúral felícity,

which Patmore quotes to point out that each of the first two syllables is equal to either of the following triplets. The lines must be filled of necessity because of the important condition inherent in metre that the measures are isochronous. Patmore gives the credit to Joshua Steele for first having discovered the "isochronous division by accents," but he dwells on the principle at length and emphasizes "the approximate equality of time between accent and accent, which, I cannot too often repeat, is the primary condition of metre in all languages." [4]

Having established his law and its conditions, Patmore goes on to discuss the nature of the two "prose" feet within the dipodic measure. He points out that it is not necessary for both to be of the same kind: frequently a measure will be mixed, containing one trochaic and one dactylic foot, to avoid the monotony of a series of identical feet. But more important, these two feet have a certain stress relationship with each other. The following lines are his illustrative quotation and his comment upon it:

> The crów doth sing as swéetly as the lárk
> When néither is atténded; and I thínk
> The níghtingale, if shé should sing by dáy
> When évery goose is cáckling, would be thóught
> No bétter a musícian than the wrén.

"In these blank trimeters, properly read, there is a major and a minor accent in every section but one." [5] In other words, normally, although not always, there will be a secondary accent within the measure, and that secondary accent will, of course, fall on the important syllable of the second "prose" foot.

This sentence of Patmore's comment, however, bears further examination. Beginning, like the verse quoted above, with a syllable of anacrusis, the measures here show an interesting pattern: "In thése blank trímeters, próperly réad, there is a májor and a minor áccent in évery section but óne." At first glance, one discovers that three of these measures are identical with Patmore's description of "dipodic" rhythm, and on second glance one sees that three more follow the same pattern by virtue of the natural pauses—after "trimeter," "accent," and "one"

—which come in the reading. What Patmore discovered in the lines from *The Merchant of Venice* is a unit of rhythm, true enough, but a unit of prose rhythm which his own comment underlines and emphasizes. The measures of his own prose refute the first assumption of his "law" (that the unit of prose rhythm is two or three syllables), and demolish the second (that the unit of poetry is twice that of prose).

This is the important error in the logic of Patmore's theory which Hopkins perceived and corrected. That Hopkins recognized the true nature of Patmore's measure is evident when he says it "is the most natural of things. For . . . it is the rhythm of common speech and of written prose, when rhythm is perceived in them." [6] Since this measure is, then, *not* composed of two prose units, the term "dipodic" which Patmore uses is false. This is a rhythmical foot having its own integrity apparent in its individual characteristics of primary and secondary stress; it cannot be described by such terms as iambic and so forth; and most important, it cannot be contained within such measures. Patmore, in discussing the isochronous nature of metre, likens the strong accent to "a post in a chain railing [which] shall mark the end of one space, and the commencement of another." Within the space of the metrical chain railing, then, the secondary accent marks something less than the whole measure, and is of a weaker nature than the post. In a sense, it is a post knocked askew, so that the rhythm measure bounds over it to the next upright post. To indicate this individual characteristic of the new measure, Hopkins uses the peculiarly vivid and descriptive term, *sprung* rhythm. If he had expanded his comment in the Preface, he might have noted that this is also the rhythm which the ear imposes upon recurrent noises. For instance, it is the rhythm by which we interpret the sound of a passing train. A naked example of it in verse, with the last element in each measure a pause, is in one of the most popular "dipodic" poems:

Boomalay   boomalay   boomalay   boom....

Patmore does not go further in describing explicitly the relationships of the elements of his rhythm measure, but he does make some interesting comments which imply the conditions of relationship. The first of these comments has to do with metrical stress and time. "Mitford, and other writers, who have treated of Latin and Greek verse as being 'metrical' and 'temporal,' and of our own as 'rhythmical' and 'accentual,' have fallen into the strange error of not perceiving that these four epithets apply to all possible kinds of metre, as far as they really are metre . . . the only change [from classical verse] as far as regards pure *metre* . . . is that which consists in rendering 'accentual' division of time the *sole,* instead of merely the *main* source of metre." [7] The phrase " 'accentual' division of time" here is important for its implications. The main accents may mark the time divisions, but the syllables which fill the metrical space must consume certain portions of that time. As Patmore points out, the considerations of accent and time are both present in the metre. If, moreover, as Patmore insists, measures containing four syllables are isochronous with those containing five or six, it follows that the syllables in the various measures do not consume equal portions of time. Since the variation in number of syllables occurs in the unemphatic parts of the measure, it is reasonable to suppose that these parts have a fairly fixed portion of time allotted to them. In the following verse, which Patmore would call a dipodic trimeter,

I sígh the lack of mány a thing I sóught,

the "y" and "a" of "many a" are shorter in duration than any of the other syllables, but the two of them are roughly equal to one of the other slack syllables. If the slack syllables fit into a certain portion of the metrical time, the question then arises as to what that portion of time is and how it is marked off.

Present-day "dipodic" theorists, in their eagerness to divorce metrical stress from time, suggest that the metrical fence-space is divided into four equal parts:

Primary stress / thesis / secondary / thesis

Patmore however, seems to suggest something else. In his discussion of syllabic time he says: "The time occupied in the actual articulation of a syllable is not necessarily its metrical value. *The time of a syllable in combination, is that which elapses from its commencement to the commencement of the succeeding syllable;* so that the mono-syllables, a, as, ask, asks, ask'st, though requiring five degrees of time for their articulation, may have precisely the same temporal value in verse." (II, 237.) A syllable may, then, either gain or lose time in metrical combination. Two or more syllables may be compressed into the time of one, one syllable may be extended over the time of several, or the time of the same syllable may vary in relation to one next it: ". . . 'du liebst' [may constitute] a spondee, an iambus, or a trochee, according to the signification borne by the words. *The material or external element of syllabic quantity, is thus dissolved and lost in the spirituality which produces quantity instead of obeying it.*" (II, 259). That spirituality which produces quantity is, fairly clearly, the *stress* which the rhythmical pattern imposes upon a syllable. If the "du liebst" be an iambus, the "du" loses in quantity because the stress is not on it; if it be a trochee, the "du" gains in quantity because the stress is on it. Both syllables will have equal time only if both be given equal stress, a spondee. In the light of these remarks of Patmore's, the relationships of the elements within the metrical space would seem to have certain general ratios. The primary stress, marking off the measures, also dominates the measure to such a degree that it can in itself absorb the time of the whole measure. The secondary stress, while it marks off a portion of time within the measure, yet marks a lesser portion of time than does the primary stress. The thesis syllables, by Patmore's inference, have a smaller portion of time, even as they have a smaller degree of emphasis, than a stressed syllable has.

There is every evidence in Hopkins' poems that he was familiar with these details of Patmore's theory and that he observed them carefully. But there is also evidence that once more he drew logical deductions from them which Patmore had not perceived. His recognition of the nature and proportional value of secondary stress is quite clear in such lines as

> Nóthing is so béautiful as spríng,

or

> Whát is all this júice and all this jóy?

in which he used the simplest form of Patmore's measure, the form which Patmore illustrates in the quotation from *The Merchant,* with secondary stress on the strong syllable of the second "trochaic foot" in each measure. It is significant that he uses these two lines deliberately (p. 105) as "sprung" measures introducing the separate sections of the sonnet. His strong consciousness of secondary stress may also be seen in his many coinings. "Inversnaid," for example, has a number of striking ones— "rollrock highroad," "windpuff-bonnet," "wiry heathpacks," "beadbonny ash"—which are obviously there to meet the demands of secondary accent. As for the shifting time relationships of adjacent syllables, in "The Caged Skylark," Hopkins illustrates, and carefully marks, one of the examples which Patmore uses, the word "sometimes":

> Both sing sometímes the sweetest, sweetest spells,
> Yet both droop deadly sómetimes in their cells. . . .

While his comprehension of the characteristics of the measure is clear enough, on the other hand his frequent avoiding of the repetition of its full patterns is equally deliberate. Here Hopkins goes far beyond Patmore or the "dipodic" poets in his recognition of the limitations as well as of the flexibility of sprung rhythm. This perception may well account for his objection of *Piers Plowman*, from which Patmore quotes:

> I looked on my left halfe
> As the lady me taught,
> And was ware of a woman
> Worthlyith clothed,
> Purfiled with pelure
> The finest upon erthe;
> Crowned with a crowne,
> The king hath no better.

There is certainly the doggerel tendency here of which Hopkins complained, and that tendency is one inherent in sprung rhythm. As a measure of ordinary speech and prose, it is a grammatical rhythm or a sentence pattern. Hence, if it is used as a recurring metrical pattern, a basis of scansion, there will be nothing to play it against. In the poetry from which Patmore extracted it, it is played against some other underlying beat on which the poets were consciously building, and therefore it produces that "perpetual conflict between the law of the verse and the freedom of the language" which Patmore declares is essential to great poetry; but by itself it has a flat, one-dimensional quality. The serious limitation of the measure is evident in most "dipodic" poems. The rolling, often trite rhythms of "Lepanto," "Cargoes," "The Congo," and so forth are entertaining up to a point, though one would soon be surfeited with them. On the other hand, when Meredith attempted to use sprung rhythm in a serious poem, the limitations of the verse often produced an incongruous effect upon the matter:

> Beautiful she looks, like a white water-lily
> Bursting out of bud in havens of the streams.
> When from bed she rises clothed from neck to ankle
> In her long nightgown sweet as boughs of May,
> Beautiful she looks, like a tall garden lily
> Pure from the night, and splendid for the day.

Even the "dipodic" poets, however, sense the need for varying the fully cadenced measures with others in which either the primary or the secondary stress, or both, are uncadenced. The most common variation is the juxta-position of the two stresses uncadenced, as in Chester-ton's "white founts falling," in Masefield's "road rails, pig lead," in Lindsay's "fat black bucks." This particular variation is almost forced upon the poet for relief from the monotony of the regular cadence, and it is one which Hopkins uses freely. However, he went far beyond the obvious variations of the rhythm in his attempt to regain the conflict between metre and sense. In his variations, he employs all degrees of metrical syllabic time. The fol-lowing line from "The Windhover" is an interesting ex-ample of his technique:

Stirred for a/bird, -the a/chieve of, the/mastery
of the/thing!

In the first four of these sprung measures, there is a progressive uncoiling of the primary stress. In the first measure "stirred" contains not only all the time of the primary stress, but most of the time of the secondary stress also. Only the two secondary cadence syllables es-cape. In the second measure, the secondary stress is re-leased in the pause, followed again by two syllables in cadence. The third measure emphasizes the secondary stress but reduces its cadence to one syllable. Finally, the fourth measure releases the full cadence of the primary stress also. This fourth measure is one that Patmore would easily recognize as a "mixed" measure of dactyl and trochee. Hopkins uses it here as a sort of time signature for the reading of the other measures of the line, meas-ures in which he is applying the inferences of Patmore's theory though Patmore himself apparently did not recog-nize these logical refinements.

The same sort of process, though in reverse, is in the line from "Pied Beauty":

Glory be to/God for/dappled/things!

Here the first measure is the fully expanded time-signature foot, the second is the common variation of the uncadenced two stresses, the third draws all but one short syllable into the primary stress, and the fourth completes the drawing-in motion. There is no indication here that Hopkins is not conscious of the role of the secondary stress. There is, rather, every indication that he is deliberately avoiding monotonous expression of it. His diligence in avoiding the incipient weakness of sprung rhythm may be further seen in the astonishing variety which he achieves in the fourth line of each stanza of "The Deutschland," lines each of three stresses, for example:

Lord of/ living and/ dead
Thy) terror, O /Christ, O/ God
I) whirled out/ wings that/ spell
And it) crowds and it/combs to the/ fall
Glow,/ glory in/ thunder
Swings the/ stroke/ dealt
Will,/ mouthed to/ flesh-burst
And) storms/ bugle his/ fame
Two) hundred/ souls in the / round

A result of Hopkins' avoidance of the fully cadenced feet is evident in his comment: "Sprung Rhythm, as used in this book, is measured by feet of from one to four syllables, regularly, and for particular effects any number of weak or slack syllables may be used." Patmore's measures, on the other hand, were regularly of four, five, or six syllables, depending on whether they were composed of two trochaic feet, two dactylic feet, or a mixture of trochee and dactyl.

The large number of syllables involved in his measures led Patmore to place severe limitations upon the number of "dipodic" feet, and hence upon the number of primary stresses which could be contained within a line. "All English verses in common cadence are therefore dimeters, trimeters, or tetrameters, and consist, when they are full

. . . of eight, twelve or sixteen syllables. Verses in triple cadence obey the same law, only their length never . . . exceeds that of the trimeter, on account of the great number of syllables or places of syllables (twenty-four) which would be involved in a tetrameter in such cadence." Again, "dipodic" poets have apparently subscribed to this stricture. Only Hopkins appears to have made the logical connection between Patmore's separate dicta on isochronous measures, metrical syllabic time, and the number of measures possible in a line. If one syllable or two syllables can fill the time of several, there is no reason why a poet should not have as many stresses as he wishes; certainly he need not be restricted because of an unwieldly number of syllables. Hopkins' practice shows what his notes to the poems suggest, that he felt that if the rhythm is established, the other feet in the line may vary as to the number of syllables and yet keep the isochronous nature of the metre. Hence the importance of the time-signature feet which we have noted.

Patmore's preoccupation with the number of syllables in his new measure led him further to make an inaccurate generalization concerning the nature of the conventional iambic pentameter line. This line (of ten syllables) he declares to be a line of three main stresses, an incomplete trimeter, whose complete form is to be seen in the Alexandrine (twelve syllables). Hopkins' pleasure in paradox, which Bridges deplores, may clearly be seen in the many deductions which Hopkins appears to make about the nature of this line as he develops his sonnets. Conceivably, in the opening lines of two of the sonnets, Patmore could have found his trimeter verses:

> Sometimes a lantern moves along the night
> That interests our eyes. And who goes there?
> I think; where from and bound, I wonder, where,
> With, all down darkness wide, his wading light?

and

I wake and feel the fell of dark, not day.
What hours, O what black hours we have spent
This night. what sights you, heart, saw; ways you went!
And more must; in yet longer light's delay.

At any rate, there would not be greater distortion in so scanning the lines than there is in Patmore's scansion of the lines from *The Merchant of Venice*.

However, it is quite impossible to make trimeters of the verses in "The Windhover," and here we come upon one of Hopkins' departures from Patmore's conclusions. Since the men who wrote in iambic pentameters were consciously building on five beats, Hopkins apparently felt that it would be reasonable in sprung rhythm to keep the five-beat idea and build sonnets of sprung pentameter verses. This verse basis is the one Hopkins uses in "The Windhover." He makes the five-beat verse pattern clear by the simple, strongly marked measures of the first line, and then goes on to develop it:

I) caught this/ morning/ morning's/ minion,/ kingdom
    of/ daylight's dauphin,/ dapple-dawn-drawn/
    Falcon, in his/ riding
Of the/ rolling/ level underneath him/ steady/ air,
    and/ striding/
High there, how he/ rung upon the/ rein of a/
    wimpling/ wing
In his/ecstasy! . . .

He describes this as "falling Paeonic rhythm," and it is worth noting that in the elaborated lines he is careful to establish the fully cadenced time-signature feet ("dapple-dawn-drawn," "Falcon in his," "High there, how he," "rung upon the") which in turn govern the reading of the first line. But Hopkins carries his consideration of the original sonnet line still further. If the usual ten syllables are merely an incomplete Alexandrine, then the true basis of the line is a six-beat rhythm. This deduction Hopkins illustrates in his sonnet "Henry Purcell," which he notes is "Alexandrine: six stresses to the line":

Have) fair/ fallen, O/ fair,/ fair have/ fallen, so/ dear
To me, so/ arch-e/ special a/ spirit as/ heaven in/
                                                    Henry/ Purcell....

More often among his sonnets, however, there seems to be a bewildering variety in the number of feet within his verses. In "Duns Scotus's Oxford," for instance, the first line has three or possibly four feet, the second certainly has five, and the last line just as certainly has four:

> Towery city and branchy between towers;
> Cuckoo-echoing, bell-swarmed, lark-charmed, rook-racked
>   river-rounded. ...
> Who fired France for Mary without spot.

In this matter, again, Hopkins shows a more perceptive study of metrical characteristics than does Patmore. As his sonnet to Bridges shows, within the conventional sonnet he has observed lines with three main stresses, lines with four main stresses, and lines with five main stresses. Indeed, this poem is almost a dissertation on variety of line within the sonnet form. The following verses from it illustrate the variety which he displays:

>   she long
> Within her wears, bears, cares and moulds the same: ...
> O then if in my lagging lines you miss
> The roll, the rise, the carol, the creation,
> My winter world, that scarcely breathes that bliss
> Now, yields you, with some sighs, our explanation.

This sonnet is conventional in the sense that, except for its fourth line, it could be scanned in the usual iambic fashion, and this fact Hopkins seems to be pointing out, half-ironically, half-disconsolately, to Bridges. In his own sonnets, he is merely applying to sprung rhythm the same abundance of variations which he found everywhere in English sonnets. However, if he is showing Bridges that his sprung measures are only employing traditional variations, he is also illustrating the weakness of Patmore's "law" about the measure of poetry. The iambic pentameter line is not simply a trimeter, a line of three main stresses; it has great elasticity of stress which does not allow of the mechanical counting of alternate accents which is the basis of Patmore's "dipodic" theory. Hopkins shows that poetic measure is much more complicated than Patmore's simple rule implies.

The sonnet provided Hopkins with a medium within which great freedom and flexibility were familiar. They were possible, as they had always been possible, because of the clear disciplines of the outer form both in rhyme scheme and in the divisions of octet and sestet, or theme and resolution. Within his verses, not only does he indicate the relationships of time by the key measure, but as Mr. Whitehall points out, he also employs devices of "constant alliteration, assonance, internal rhyme, and word repetition," that bring out the inner structure. However, in a rhythm as free as that which Hopkins strove for, the further discipline of outer form is essential to the full realization of the internal music. Here again is a conception of poetic composition, though not at all a new one, which appears in the "Essay on English Metrical Law." Patmore points out that Hegel, "whose chapters on music and metre" are the philosophic basis for his theory, maintains that the substitution of accentual division of time for true syllabic quantity necessitates an outer force which will have the function of a time-marker. This function is fulfilled by "rhyme . . . of which the very grossness, as compared with syllabic quantity, is a great advantage" (p. 259). Furthermore, rhyme is "a means of indefinitely extending the limits, and multiplying the symmetry of measure by the formation of stanzas." Stanzas, then, in themselves add to the many tangible and intangible elements which go to make up the music, law, and proportion of poetry. There is, moreover, a further consideration involved in stanza form. It is that of run-on scansion, which both Patmore and Hopkins champion. The verse has its individual metrical purpose, but that purpose is subordinated to the theme of the whole unit, which must be sufficiently limited in scope to allow the melody pattern to remain clear. Such pattern is important in Hopkins' conception of his poems. The sonnets are carefully and elaborately built musical statements. Sometimes the statement is one long melody; sometimes it is broken into phrases of 4, 4, 3, 3, verses; sometimes it consists of theme and one or more "codas." In his longer poems, in which the form is not marked by the peculiar structure of the sonnet, the stanzas are carefully used to "multiply the symmetry of measure." Of "The Loss of the Eurydice," Hopkins says, "each stanza is rather one long line rhymed in passage than four lines with rhymes at the ends." These long lines, symmetrical in pattern, become the variations on the theme as they add to and enforce the opening statement. The idea of variation on a theme comes out most clearly, perhaps in the meticulously built up stanza form of "The Deutschland," in which the image of the hourglass, which Mr. Mizener shows is an important one, [8] seems to be presented to the ear. Rhyme and therefore stanza form (for Patmore excludes the couplet as producing inferior poetry) are accepted by both Patmore and Hopkins as having inherent aesthetic value. Certainly there was no barrier between the two men here as Mr. Whitehall suggests there was when he says that Hopkins' "concessions to stanzaic form" hindered his comprehension of Patmore. Hopkins' practice in his concern with stanza forms shows rather an agreement with Patmore's values.

While Hopkins agrees with Patmore in the matters of rhyme and stanza, of isochronous measures and of syllabic time, his differences with him are significant ones. He first places the new measure on its true foundation as a rhythm of "common speech and written prose," rather than on Patmore's curious and unreliable "dipodic" rule. He breaks through the inflexibility of Patmore's strictures on the number of measures which may be contained in a single line of poetry. He shows the fallibility of Patmore's observations on the iambic pentameter line, and in the process he produces the most convincing rebuttal of all the terms of Patmore's law. Nevertheless, he uses Patmore's measure forcefully, subtly, brilliantly as a rhythmic basis of verse.

III

Behind Patmore's admiration for rhyme, stanza form, and "dipodic" measure, there are a number of aesthetic ideas, to some of which Hopkins apparently subscribed, for a time at any rate. One of Patmore's beliefs was in the early and continually desirable identification of poetry and music. As a result, he develops an aesthetic which postulates that the poetry which most closely approaches that which it is not, music, is the highest of its kind. His scale of values is apparent in the latter part of his statement that "the co-ordination of life and law, in the matter and form of poetry, determines the different degrees and kinds of metre, from the half-prosaic dramatic verse to the extremest elaboration of high lyric metres" (II, 221). Pursuing his musical analogy as the basis for judgment of poetry, Patmore finds that "in verses which strike the ear as extraordinarily musical, the peculiarity is mainly owing to an unusually distinct and emphatic accentuation of the first syllable in the metrical section" (II, 245).

Hopkins makes clear what this judgment is based on when he says that it is convenient in scanning poetry to take the stress first "as the accent or the chief accent always comes first in a musical bar." Both men are basing poetic judgments, and present-day "dipodic" theorists follow them, on the musical convention of the bar system. There is here, surely, a curious anachronism. Both men are trying to establish universal metrical principles, and yet they base their attempts on a late arising musical convention which is in no sense universal. Almost as soon as the bar system was firmly established for the guidance of the various voices and instruments, in the late sixteenth and early seventeenth centuries, there began to develop the special vocabulary and signs by which musicians try to overcome its tyranny. Composers further developed the system of changing time-signature within their compositions in order to allow for free variation in rhythm and tempo. Then came the unusual measures of 5/4, 7/8 time, and eventually some modern composers abandoned the bar divisions altogether in order to emphasize larger patterns of symmetry and proportion. Yet both Patmore and Hopkins erect this musicians' convenience, with its tendency to place the strong accent on the first beat, into a fundamental law of poetry, and use it as a standard of aesthetic judgment. That they are uneasy about this is indicated when they both insist that there are rising rhythms as well as falling rhythms in poetry, which distinctions, says Hopkins, "are real and true to nature." Nevertheless, when they come to apply the musical analogy to the more minute measures of poetry, the effect is to eliminate rising rhythms altogether. Patmore's examples are all given in terms of trochees and dactyls, and Hopkins says quite bluntly that if the musical custom is followed in the scanning of poetry "there will be in common English verse only two possible feet—the so-called accentual Trochee and Dactyl, and correspondingly only two possible rhythms, the so-called Trochaic and Dactylic."

This conclusion is an odd one in view of the dominance of the iambic pentameter line from Chaucer to Bridges. Patmore circumvents any possible impasse in an ingenious fashion. Those poets who thought they were writing iambic pentameters either were unconsciously writing "dipodic" trimeters or else they were poor poets; only Milton is an exception to the rule. In his judgments, Patmore claps nineteenth-century taste on poetic virtue. He discovers that the poetry which is the most musical, and therefore the highest in degree, has a falling note and moreover can be pressed into his new measures. That poetry which does not show such qualities is either "half-prosaic dramatic verse" or, worse still, "Pope's couplet."

Of the couplet, Patmore says with an air of triumph: "The fault of this couplet is not only its essentially epigrammatic character, which is but a relative defect; it is, furthermore, absolutely faulty, inasmuch as the combination of immediately recurrent rhyme, with the long final pause, gives an emphasis contrasting too strongly with the very weak accentual construction of the line, which, as it is ordinarily treated, has no sectional—i.e., 'dipodal'—division" (II, 261). He is thus able, from the basis of his theory of what poetry ought to be, to reject the works of the eighteenth century; however, Patmore prefaces these remarks with the somewhat surprising comment that "the heroic measure of Chaucer and his successors [was] regarded as fit only for humorous subjects." Having disposed of the couplet and dramatic blank verse, he approaches the problem of non-dramatic blank verse. His great admiration for Milton, "who first taught us what this kind of verse ought to be," affords him an easy way out of his difficulty here. Only "the transcendent genius of Milton" was able to achieve the metrically improbable, great poetry in iambic pentameters. This happy coincidence of contemporary taste with poetic theory no doubt appealed to Hopkins also, for, as Mr. Mizener points out, much of Hopkins' thinking as a poet "is that of the typical 19th century Englishman." Yet the difficulty of reconciling "dipodic" theory and the evidence of the English poetic tradition does exist, and it is possible that Hopkins' eventual recognition of it lies behind the apparent capitulation to convention in his later poems. It is also possible that the more he came to know about music, the clearer appeared the fallacy of submitting poetry to its laws and conventions.

Bridges says: "It is lamentable that Gerard Hopkins died when, to judge by his latest work, he was beginning to concentrate the force of all his luxuriant experiments in rhythm and diction, and castigate his art into a more reserved style." Yet among the later poems are "Harry Ploughman" and "Heraclitean Fire," which show little evidence of castigation. Neither does Hopkins' note on the sonnet "Alfonsus": "The sonnet (I say it snorting) aims at being intelligible." He has not abandoned sprung rhythm, but the other late poems suggest that he is willing to admit other rhythms. Sprung rhythm, or "dipodic" rhythm, is not the only rhythm in poetry, nor yet possibly is it the music of the spheres.

NOTES

1 Kenyon Critics (ed.), *Gerard Manley Hopkins* (Norfolk, Conn: New Directions Press, 1945), p. 37.

2 Robert Bridges (ed.), *Poems of Gerard Manley Hopkins* (2nd. ed.; London: Oxford University Press, 1930), p. 102.

3 Coventry Patmore, *Poems* (London, 1890), II, 242. All italics quoted from Patmore are his own.

4 *Ibid.,* II, 249. Mr. Whitehall makes a curious statement: "Hopkins had stumbled upon a basic but hitherto unrecognized principle of rhythm—English or foreign, classical or modern. Consciously or unconsciously, he had come to realize that a metrical foot represents a unit in a series of even-time (isochronous) units and that . . . their time-lapses may be occupied by anything from a single heavy-stressed syllable to four or five syllables." (Kenyon Critics, p. 36).

5 Patmore, II, 245.

6 Hopkins, *Poems,* p. 5.

7 Patmore, II, 235-36. Further references to Patmore's *Poems* and Hopkins' *Poems* are cited in the text rather than in footnotes, the former book being indicated by volume and page, the latter by page only.

8 Arthur Mizener, "Victorian Hopkins" in Kenyon Critics, p. 111.

Elgin W. Mellown

THE RECEPTION OF GERARD MANLEY
HOPKINS' POETRY, 1889-1930 [1]

I

A number of Gerard Manley Hopkins' poems had already
been published when his friend Robert Bridges edited the
first collection in 1918. The early publications and the
1918 *Poems* passed almost unnoticed by the poetry-read-
ing public, and it was not until the second edition of the
Poems was published in 1930 that Hopkins came to be
widely known. His subsequent importance and influence
can be explained in part by examining the reception of
his work between 1889 and 1930.

During Hopkins' lifetime he published nine minor
poems or translations, and he was known to some of his
Oxford acquaintances as a poet. After his death Bridges
was intrusted with his manuscript poems, to deal with
them as he saw fit. His first publication of Hopkins was
in 1893 in A. H. Miles' *Poets and Poetry of the Nineteenth Century,* Volume VIII. In January, 1893, Miles
visited Bridges at Yattendon to make arrangements concerning the latter's contributions to the anthology, and
Bridges persuaded him to include ten poems by Hopkins
as well. Bridges wrote the introductory "Notice," com-
bining biographical information with blunt criticism. The
"Notice" was for many years the chief source of published information concerning Hopkins, and the ten poems
composed the primary collection of his poetry before
1918. There were several editions of the Miles anthology
before 1900.

Several poems were published separately in the 1890s.
The *Stonyhurst Magazine* printed a letter (Feb., 1894)

from "O. S. J." which contained the poem "Ad Mariam," and the *Irish Monthly* (Dublin: May, 1898) published "Rosa Mystica." "Mary, Mother of Divine Grace, Compared to the Air We Breathe" was included in the *Book of Christmas Verse* in 1895 by the editor, H. C. Beeching, a nephew-in-law of Bridges who had met Hopkins in 1887. He edited another anthology in 1895, *Lyra Sacra,* in which he printed four poems by Hopkins, repeating one from Miles' volume. Thus by 1900 seventeen poems were available in publications ranging from a school paper to a popular anthology.

These poems won Hopkins his first admirers. Charles Williams wrote in *Time and Tide* (Feb. 3, 1945) that his first reading of Hopkins had been from "two or three pages torn from one of those little red volumes known as the *Poets and Poetry of the Century.*" He and his friends "read . . . admired . . . were thrilled." Other young men who knew Bridges were given the opportunity to read the poems in manuscript. Visitors to Bridges at Yattendon, and later in Oxford, were often shown them, according to Mrs. Lascelles Abercrombie; her husband was "tremendously struck with them." [2] Another poet who visited Bridges at Yattendon was Laurence Binyon; in 1890 he read some of the "tragic" sonnets which "greatly impressed" him, although he confessed, fifty years later (in "Gerard Hopkins and His Influence," *UTQ,* VIII [1939], 264), that had he read any of the more difficult poems at that time he would "probably . . . not have appreciated" them. Yet another visitor to Yattendon was Roger Fry, a cousin of Mrs. Bridges. To him, Hopkins' poems appeared to be greater than those of Tennyson, and to his poet-friend R. C. Trevelyan he wrote: "I've got some manuscript poems by Gerald [sic] Hopkins which would make you tear your hair. Look at this: 'I caught this morning morning's minion-king,' etc." (Virginia Woolf, *Roger Fry: A Biography* [1940], pp. 84-5).

In 1900 Basil Champneys gave additional biographical information in his *Memoirs and Correspondence of Cov-*

entry Patmore. Champneys pointed out Hopkins' influence on the older poet and how he encouraged Patmore to write the account of his conversion; Champneys also reported the frequently discussed incident of Patmore's destroying his religious meditations because Hopkins said to him, "That's telling secrets" (I, 175, 1, 318). Champneys printed nine of Hopkins' letters to Patmore. In 1902 Orby Shipley reprinted "Rosa Mystica" and "Mary, Mother of Divine Grace" in his massive *Carmina Mariana.* In this decade there was also a reference to Hopkins by Mary Elizabeth Coleridge in her "Preface" to *The Last Poems of R. W. Dixon* (1905), while the "Private Jesuit Periodical" *Letters and Notices* published extracts from his Journal in 1906 and 1907. [3]

The first separate study of Hopkins' poetry was by an American Catholic, Katherine Brégy, whose "Gerard Hopkins: An Epitaph and an Appreciation" appeared in the *Catholic World* (New York: LXXXVIII [Jan., 1909], 433-47; reprinted in Miss Brégy's *The Poets' Chantry* [1912]). She referred only to the poems in Miles', Shipley's, and Beeching's anthologies and was apparently unaware of those Bridges held, for she wrote: "His poems are scattered in a few precious anthologies, still awaiting the zeal of collector and editor. It seems probable, unless he himself destroyed them during the last years, that a number of them are still somewhere in manuscript form; for of those already published, about one-third have been given in this article." Miss Brégy's approach was biographical and directed to the Catholic reader. She was concerned that Hopkins not be dismissed as an amateur, declaring of the sonnet "Spring" that "It was written in 1877 and its existence argues for Father Hopkins more than a mere dilettante use of the poetical faculty." Although she did not know the more difficult poems, she could see that "Lucidity was the chief grace he sacrificed as years wore on; and his fondness for uncommon words—at one moment academic and literate, at another provincial—did not help matters." Her estimate of Hopkins' reputation in 1909 was that "Outside of the poets . . . [his] work has had no recognition and no understanding."

Six months later the *Month* published articles in July, August, and September by Father Joseph Keating, S.J., entitled "Impressions of Father Gerard Hopkins, S.J." (CXIV, 59-68, 151-60, 246-58). Concerned largely with Hopkins' reputation during his life, Keating quoted excerpts from letters received by Hopkins from Newman, Pusey, Patmore, and others; no poems were included, although Keating urged the publication of a complete edition: "It would seem that the time has now come for Father Hopkins' poems to appear in a collected form as a distinct and valuable addition to the literary heritage of the Catholic Church." He knew of the manuscript poems, and he made several references to them. His remarks prompted Bridges to write to him on October 14, 1909, evidently about his guardianship. Of those poems already published, he declared that his "selection was carefully made so that only what was likely to be well received should be seen. I went as far as I dared and my judgement has been justified by the result." [4] One might note, however, that in Bridges' editions of the *Poems by the Late Reverend Richard Watson Dixon* (1909) and the *Poems of Digby Mackworth Dolben* (1911) there is no mention of Hopkins' poetic talents, notwithstanding the many references to him.

Hopkins was also mentioned in widely circulated books in these years. George Saintsbury included his former Oxford contemporary in his three-volume *A History of English Prosody* (1910). The paragraph concerning him (which remained unchanged in the 1923 edition) concluded: "he never published any; and it is quite clear that all were experiments." The 1912 *Oxford Book of Victorian Verse*, edited by Arthur Quiller-Couch, included "The Starlight Night;" no information was given about the author.

Hopkins' undergraduate life at Oxford was one of several subjects in a long personal recollection by the Rev.

W. L. Lechmere for the *Oxford and Cambridge Review* (May, 1912). Lechmere showed no knowledge of Hopkins' poetry; rather he remembered his "superfineness of mind and character." But Father Keating knew of the poems, and in the *Month* (CXXI [June, 1913], 643-44) he described Hopkins as "a diligent polisher of his own productions, as well as a valued critic," and pointedly asked that the poems be published.

The second long study of the poetry also came from America. Alfred Joyce Kilmer's essay in *Poetry* (Chicago: IV [Sept., 1914], 241-45) was the most discerning of any of these early studies. "It is the overwhelming greatness of his theme that justifies the lavishness of his method," Kilmer wrote, and related Hopkins to one of his Oxford influences by saying: "Walter Pater . . . had no keener sensitivity to the color and music of language." Although Kilmer knew only a few of the poems, his insight was remarkable: "There will always be those who dislike the wealth of imagery which characterizes Gerard Hopkins's poetry, because they do not understand his mental and spiritual attitude." To him, Hopkins was "the most scrupulous word-artist of the nineteenth-century." This article in *Poetry,* then a magazine of the avant-garde, marked the first time that Hopkins' work was discussed for readers interested in him primarily as a poet.

In January, 1916, Bridges included six Hopkins poems in his anthology *The Spirit of Man.* Editions of this popular anthology were published as late as the Second World War. Volume XIII of the *Cambridge History of English Literature* also appeared in 1916 with the chapter on "Lesser Poets" written by Saintsbury, who considered Hopkins in a footnote as a "contemporary of Lang at Oxford" and dismissed him as having "developed partially acute, but not generally sound, notions on metre." Passing references to him were made in 1916 by Thomas MacDonagh in his nationalistic *Literature in Ireland,* and by Sister M. P. Neenan, in her Catholic University (Washington) dissertation, *Some Evidences of Mysticism in English Poetry of the Nineteenth Century.*

At least once before 1918 Hopkins was mentioned in a widely circulated periodical: the *New Statesman* on June 9, 1917, printed an essay on his life and poetry by J. M. Hone (IX, 231-32). He was described as "a poet of distinction and originality" who had developed and practiced "spring [sic] rhythm." Hone's insight was shown as he placed Hopkins in historical perspective: "Striving after an impossible subtlety of expression, absorbed in theory of form and of rhythm, detaching his matter from all subjects of temporary interest or of a speculative character, he was in reaction against most of the literary influences of the nineteenth century; even Tennyson appeared to him as a 'great outsider,' not a companion of the craft." Hone deplored the fact that only some twenty poems had been published. An interesting response to this article was a letter from Hall Caine (June 23, 1917, p. 277) who felt that Hone, in referring to his excluding some sonnets by Hopkins from an 1881 anthology, had questioned his literary taste. Hopkins was also the subject of a short essay by Aloysius J. Hogan, S.J., in the Catholic weekly *America* (New York: Feb. 16, 1918), and was mentioned briefly by H. C. Beeching in a note which he wrote for T. H. Ward's *The English Poets,* Volume V (1918).

Roughly half these notices occurred in works of Roman Catholic origin or appeal. A few references were in specialized works concerning prosody: in this field he was rarely understood and often curtly dismissed, but of course few of his poems were available to critics. To the admirers of Coventry Patmore, as well as to the limited audiences of Dixon and Dolben, Hopkins was known as a priest and a critic, but not as a poet. Although his poetry appeared in six anthologies before 1918, the only representative selection was that in Miles' volume. By slowly releasing the poems to the public, Bridges aroused some interest in them, even, according to C. C. Abbott, that of the eventual publisher, Humphrey Milford. [5] A small audience awaited the *Poems,* an essentially conservative group composed largely of prosodists and Catholic poetry lovers whose appreciation of Hopkins was due either to a limited knowledge of the poetry or religious sympathy for the poet.

II

The reaction of the literary public of 1919 to the *Poems* was influenced by several factors, the popularity of Bridges being foremost. His appointment to the Laureateship in 1913 had occasioned much outspoken criticism, for he was considered a coterie poet of what is now labeled the "Establishment"; but such adverse criticism had been disarmed in 1916 by his editing *The Spirit of Man* and by his patriotic wartime writings. He could have endorsed the poetry in such a way that its approval would have been assured. However, his "Preface to Notes" allowed him to state his objections to Hopkins' verse and his prejudices against his friend's religion; and concern for the recognition of the poems did not temper his forthright statements. The "Preface" clearly showed his opinion that the poetry was to be valued for the occasional beauty of the novel technique and for its unfulfilled promise; and, since the "Preface" set the critical tone of many reviews, it must be accounted a chief influence on the reception of the *Poems.* Another influential factor was Hopkins' religion. As a Roman Catholic he was grouped by many readers with the not inconsiderable number of Catholic poets of the late nineteenth and early twentieth centuries and was accepted or ignored on this basis alone. Even more important was the fact that he was a Victorian and hence a part of the society which progressive moderns hoped had been ended by the war. Before he could be accepted, there had to be such a dialectical process as actually took place in the 1920s and '30s, which made him a "modern" poet for "modern" readers.

The appearance of the *Poems of Gerard Manley Hopkins Now First Published* was in keeping with the conservative audience which first read the volumes: the paper was of the best quality, and there were four excellent reproductions of photographs and manuscripts. Only 750 copies of this edition were printed (there was only one impression); [6] they were priced at twelve shillings and sixpence, roughly two or three times the average cost of a book of poetry in 1919. Review copies were sent out in late December, 1918, the subsequent reviews falling into two categories, those in publications having a general appeal and those in Catholic publications.

Reviews in non-sectarian journals began with the *Glasgow Herald* (Jan. 2, 1919, p. 3), and a week later the volume was given a full-page review in the *Times Literary Supplement* (Jan. 9, 1919, p. 19) by Arthur Clutton-Brock. [7] He was very likely acquainted with Hopkins' work before reading the *Poems;* for through his association with Bridges, H. C. Beeching, Andrew Lang, and George Saintsbury, who all wrote for the *Supplement* and had read the poetry in manuscript, he would have had opportunities to read and discuss it with his fellow critics. The informed tone of his essay suggests that he had been prepared for the *Poems* and that his ideas had not been formed in the previous fortnight. He felt that Hopkins had "heard everywhere a music too difficult, because too beautiful, for our ears and noted down what he could catch of it; authentic fragments that we could trust even when they bewilder us." He also found an intellectual content in the verses: "For Hopkins poetry meant difficulty; he wrote it to say more than could be said otherwise; it was for him a packing of words with sense, both emotional and intellectual. The defect of the newest English poetry is that it says too little." The reviewer quietly defended the poet against one of Bridges' charges: "Hopkins' verse . . . assumes that the reader grasps the sense of what is unsaid. He begins where most poets leave off, not out of affectation, but because he wishes to go further." The poems, Clutton-Brock advised, were "best read aloud; then the very sense becomes clearer and anyone with an ear can hear that the method is not affectation but eagerness to find an expression for the depths of the mind, for things hardly yet consciously thought or felt." [8] Readers of this review would certainly have felt encouraged to buy the book.

Clutton-Brock's review was independent and justly critical. Other reviewers agreed with Bridges' attitude: Michael Henry, writing in *Everyman* (XIII, [Feb. 8, 1919], 416-17), forthrightly stated his debt to the editor, declaring that "this edition [is] a final one. The critic must be conscious that a master has been before him with his task when he turns to the Editor's modest 'Preface to Notes' on the *Poems,* and learns thus in what spirit the valuation of Hopkins's achievement must be attempted." Henry was one of the first critics to note the similarity of Hopkins and "the men of the seventeenth century whose life centered in religion," but he maintained Bridges' hypercritical tone, even selecting the "most unblemished poems" —"Binsey Poplars" and "The Leaden Echo and the Golden Echo." The reviewer politely demurred at the price of the volume; and obviously the cost restricted circulation.

The author of the unsigned review in the *New Statesman* (XII [March 15, 1919], 530) was Edward Shanks. [9] To him the poetry was "to eye, ear, and mind the strangest that has been published in England—the poetry of Mr. Doughty not excepted—in modern times." A conservative poet himself, Shanks agreed with Bridges' criticism: the "Beauties" of the verse, he wrote, "are scattered and they are never far from extravagant uglinesses. A perfect line is exceedingly rare; and a poem which is good as a whole, even in spite of faults, is hard to discover." Hopkins, he felt, could be but a minor influence on English verse: "a few poets will discover, absorb and render again the little which Hopkins had to offer to English verse, either in new rhythms or the free and vigorous use of epithet."

The attitude of subsequent reviewers in the *Spectator* (CXXII [May 10, 1919], 599), the *Oxford Magazine,* the *Methodist Recorder* (May 29, 1919, p. 2), and the *Dial* was no less critical. In the *Oxford Magazine* (XXXVII [May 23, 1919], 310-11) the anonymous reviewer felt that while Hopkins had evidently written for more than the "desultory reader," his poems would be confused with the work of modern poets which was "unintelligible through sheer indiscipline and carelessness"; and the sonnet "Harry Ploughman" was unfavorably compared to Masefield's "sketch of the ploughman at the end of 'The Everlasting Mercy.' " In the *Dial* (New York: LXVI [May 31, 1919], 572), the reviewer emphasized that the subject matter was "too prevailingly theological to gain a wide reading" and that the style had "a teasing quaintness, an antique tone oddly incongrous with the time of publication."

The *Athenaeum* review was by its editor, John Middleton Murry (June 6, 1919 [No. 4649, pp. 425-6]; later included in his *Aspects of Literature* [1920]), who studied the poems with care. Hopkins' poetry, he felt, was "preeminently the music of song, the music most proper to lyrical verse." Guided by this idea, he decided that "a technical progression onwards from the 'Skylark' is accordingly the main line of Hopkins' poetical evolution." The "tyranny" of this musical principle was responsible for the obscurity of the earlier verse; such obscurity was avoided only in the later sonnets where the "urgency of the content" overcame the musical elaboration. Yet "Hopkins was not the man to feel, save on exceptional occasions, that urgency of content. . . . The communication of thought was seldom the dominant impulse of his creative moment, and it is curious how simple his thought often proves to be when the obscurity of his language has been penetrated." Murry wrote that readers "will speculate whether the failure of his whole achievement was due to the starvation of experience which his vocation imposed upon him, or to a fundamental vice in his poetical endeavour. For ourselves we believe that the former was the true cause. His 'avant toute chose' whirling dizzily in a spiritual vacuum, met with no salutary resistance to modify, inform and strengthen it." Such remarks were influenced by the "Preface," but they came primarily from the "new" psychology of Freud and Jung which Murry was promoting, and they foreshadow the psychological criticism of Hopkins which prevailed in the 1930s.

In later reviews of the *Poems* Edward Sapir, in *Poetry* (XVIII [Sept., 1921], 330-36) appreciated Hopkins' work, even accepting the fact that he might have "loved difficulty, even obscurity, for its own sake." The review further indicates the introduction of psychoanalysis into literary criticism, for Sapir decided Hopkins was "a passionate soul unendingly in conflict. . . . A Freudian psychologist might call him an imperfectly sex-sublimated mystic." The young journalist Samuel Putnam reviewed the *Poems* in the Chicago *Evening Post* (May 30, 1924) as examples of metaphysical poetry.

The reviews in Catholic newspapers and journals show chiefly the religious temper of the times, although those written by Theodore Maynard and Louise Imogen Guiney were free from religious bias. Maynard, writing in the *New Witness* (XIII [Jan. 24, 1919], 259-60), called Hopkins "more modern than the most freakish modern would dare to be. Ezra Pound is stale set beside this poet who has been dead for thirty years. . . . He is the last word in technical development." Maynard's later review in *America* (XX [March 1, 1919], 533-4) gave the puff direct to the volume: "To the general reader of poetry, to the professional poet and to the Catholic, these poems, now published in a complete edition for the first time, will be forever one of the most valued of their possessions." [10] Miss Guiney, the American poet resident in England, was equally approving of the *Poems*. She had followed the publication of Hopkins' verse since 1894, and Humphrey Milford recognized her authority by sending her a review copy (*Letters of Louise Imogen Guiney* [1926], II, 250).

In her nine-page article in the *Month* (CXXXIII [March, 1919], 205-14), she called the editor's "anti-Roman" attitude "most irrelevant unwisdom," but stated that "we all owe Dr. Bridges a debt of profound gratitude." Her attention was focused on the poems, however, which received her sometimes effusive praise. Unlike other critics she studied and approved the "Author's Preface," wondering why Hopkins had not noticed that Donne "roves and revels and radiates in Sprung Rhythm." As Middleton Murry was to do several months later, she called attention to the music of the verse: the poet filled "every stanza, Debussy-like, with accent, slur, pause, tie, syncopation. . . . Gerard Hopkins is the most choral of English poets." Similar praise was also to be found in a shorter review which Miss Guiney wrote for the *Ave Maria* (April, 1919, pp. 433-35).

Reaction to Bridges' intemperate words about Hopkins' religion and to the omission of some of the devotional verse colored the editorials and reviews which appeared in the *Saturday Westminster Gazette* (LIII [March 8, 1919], 13-14) and the *Universe* (March 14, 1919, p. 2); and for several weeks readers of these journals were entertained by a sharply-worded controversy which was more concerned with Bridges than Hopkins. Similar attacks were also published by the *Irish Monthly* (XLVII [Aug., 1919], 441-48) and the *Catholic World* (CIX [July, 1919], 501-12).

More balanced reviews appeared in the *Tablet* (CXXXIII [April 5, 1919], 420) and *Catholic Book Notes* (XXIII [April, 1919], 52-3), where the writer referred readers to Miss Guiney as the final authority on the poet. The *Month* continued to publish material relating to Hopkins, including in the April, 1919, issue (CXXXIII, 285-9) an article by E. M. Harting on "Gerard Hopkins and Digby Dolben"; and in the May issue (339-40) the poem "Rosa Mystica" as an example of the verses omitted from the *Poems*. Peter McBrien, writing in the *Irish Rosary Literary Supplement* (Dublin:

XXIII [June, 1919], 473-8) found a similarity between Patmore, Wilde, Meredith, and Hopkins; while George O'Neill, professor of literature at the Royal University, agreed in his review for *Studies* (Dublin: VIII [June, 1919], 331-5) with Bridges' strictures about the former professor of classics: "He was a cultivated scholar, but this did not stay him from fantastic misuse of the English language." [11]

A four-part essay in the *Dublin Review* (CLXVII [July-Sept., 1920], 40-66) added pertinent biographical information to that already published. It was by Frederick Page, who wrote the literary criticism, and a consortium of writers under the name "Plures," who gave biographical details. These writers cannot be identified, but Shane Leslie, editor of the *Review,* was probably prominent among them. Page's criticism was not outstanding, but the biography gave details made generally available only in 1930 with the publication of Father Lahey's *Gerard Manley Hopkins,* and in 1935, 1937, and 1938, when the letters and journals were published. The implicit attitude was that Hopkins was a divided personality in whom the poet warred against the priest. Relying upon the memories of those who had known Hopkins in Dublin, "Plures" related incidents of his unhappiness in Dublin and considered him a failure as a teacher and even as a Jesuit. "Many Catholics," they recalled, "thought he had mistaken his vocation." But, "the Society loved him for his delicate scruples and holy remorse, and because he was the quintessence of the priest, sincerely dead to himself." Unlike Pater and "a generation of callow poets," Hopkins chose, "though he could not have preferred, the lonely and unresponsive corridors of a Jesuit house, and he instructed an amused and unadoring class in Hellenic metre."

One can see then that Bridges' "Preface" was the most important influence on the immediate reception of the *Poems.* Although some critics strove toward original criticism, the majority (including those who attacked Bridges) were guided by his personal attitudes. In 1890 he had written to the poet's mother to explain his delay in editing the poems and to tell of his plans for "a short preface which 'should put the poems out of the reach of criticism.' "[12] When he actually published the Preface, its effect was almost exactly what he had desired, although he probably did not foresee the judgment that the poet was a "modern" born before his time. This attitude generally resulted from syllogistic reasoning by critics who liked the verse and, not being able to accept a Victorian author, were forced to make him into a "modern." Most critics, however, were content to place him in the generation of their fathers and, at the price of twelve and six for his work, to leave him there.

III

To appreciate the phenomenal success of the second edition of the *Poems* (1930), one must trace the growth of Hopkins' reputation in the 1920s. At least nine anthologies of the decade included his poems, but over half were published after 1925, and his inclusion thus indicates a growing interest rather than being a cause of such interest. His work was also to be found in studies like Evelyn Underhill's *Essentials of Mysticism* (1920), as well as in such textbooks as T. S. Omond's *English Metrists* (1921)—where the poems were sneeringly dismissed—and G. N. Shuster's *Catholic Spirit in Modern Literature* (New York, 1922). Writers like Theodore Maynard (in *Our Best Poets, English and American* [1924]) and Osbert Burdett (in *The Beardsley Period* [1925]) used his poems as examples of technical experiment, while Anne Tuell (in *Mrs. Meynell and Her Literary Generation* [1925]) saw them merely in relation to contemporary Catholic poetry.

Such "historical" references neither influenced Hopkins' reception nor indicated contemporary appreciation of him, but other literary works emanating from Oxford and Cambridge were influential. The publication of the *Poems* coincided with the return to the universities of men older and maturer than the average undergraduate. Among this wartime generation was Alan Porter, who studied Hopkins in connection with Coventry Patmore, and who, according to Professor J. Isaacs, a friend of Porter at Oxford, was one of the first men there to appreciate the *Poems*. His interest is evident in an essay which he wrote in 1923 for the *Spectator* (CXXX [Jan. 13, 1923], 66). It began with the appraisal that Hopkins' poems "are known mainly to students of prosody and to the youngest generation of poets." Porter was concerned with explication, finding that the poet's "difficulties are necessary: they are the impress of himself. He was a man of heightened, almost hysterical, acuteness of sense." His "scholarship in Latin" was responsible for his treatment of English as if it were an inflected language, resulting in his creation of "an idiom of his own."

The quality of Porter's criticism indicates that he and his contemporaries had more than a facile appreciation of Hopkins. They included, among others, Robert Graves and Edmund Blunden. While Blunden did not write any signed criticism of Hopkins in the decade, Graves collaborated in writing the most influential study to come from Oxford. In *A Survey of Modernist Poetry* (1927) Graves and Laura Riding unequivocally labeled Hopkins a "modernist" because the words of his poetry *"had to be understood as he meant them to be, or understood not at all"* (p. 90). Treating the poems in the same manner as those by E. E. Cummings, T. S. Eliot, and John Crowe Ransom, they analysed language and technique in detail. Since *A Survey* was both an apologia and a manifesto for "modernist" poetry, Hopkins' work appealed to Graves and Miss Riding because it had been attacked by Bridges and other Georgians and thus provided an opportunity for a counterattack. The authors' assumption that an audience attracted to modern verse would be familiar with Hopkins' name and poetry is significant.

To such undergraduate poets as Auden, Day Lewis, and MacNeice, who later wrote poems influenced by Hopkins, this announcement of the poet's modernity must have been impressive; and Graves' later comment that "certain carefree paragraphs in *A Survey*" led to the "rapid exhaustion of the stagnant original edition" is probably true. [13]

At Cambridge Hopkins was taken up by such controversial lecturers as I. A. Richards: writing for the *Dial* (LXXXI [Sept., 1926], 195-203) he accepted Hopkins almost without reservation. Considering for example his verbal obscurity, Richards declared that it was intentional: "The more the poems are studied, the clearer it becomes that their oddities are always deliberate. They may be aberrations, they are not blemishes." He found that Hopkins' practice bolstered his own critical theories, for the poet "uses words always as tools, an attitude towards them which the purist and grammarian can never understand," while Hopkins himself provided a laboratory specimen for Richards' psychological theories, his demand for a "transvaluation of values." This essay indicates why the "new" critics were to give so much attention to Hopkins: his poems were not known because of their "obscurity," which had been labeled "willful." If Bridges' adjective was correct, these critics seem to have reasoned, should the poems not be examined as fulfilling the poet's intentions rather than dismissed as frustrating the reader's anticipation? Critics found the poems could be used for almost any purpose; and thus Hopkins' work inevitably came under their special scrutiny.

Such followers of Richards as Alec Brown relied even more strongly on the new psychology. In "Gerard Hopkins and Associative Form" (*Dublin Magazine,* III [April-June, 1928], 6-21), Brown declared that "the recent sudden development of psychological insight" made possible the establishment of "a complete and final poetics." Similar avowals had been made by other writers in the decade, but Brown was the first to treat Hopkins from this point of view. Lacking biographical information, however, he was forced to make deductions from the poems, stressing the thesis that "Hopkins . . . was striving, even in his most complicated passages, after grammatical logic, whereas the other logic [*i.e.,* cumulative association], that which is the potential basis of all poetry, came naturally from him; though without the advantage of control . . . we thus find, beside the most halting of ordinary verse, the extreme expression to the extent the logico-grammatical framework he clung to allowed, of associative logic." While many of Brown's conclusions are doubtful, they are interesting historically as self-conscious attempts toward Richards' desired "change in belief, the mental attitude, itself."

Richards continued to bring Hopkins' poems before his classes at Cambridge, using them in the tests of literary appreciation discussed in *Practical Criticism* (1929). His students' comments ("protocols") on "Spring and Fall" included here provide a sample of undergraduate reaction to Hopkins. Predictably they reveal either a willingness to accept "difficult" poetry or preformed attitudes that prevented such acceptance. None of them indicates any previous knowledge of Hopkins. Richards' students considered him (to quote Christopher Isherwood [*Lions and Shadows,* 1938]) "infinitely more than a brilliant new literary critic: he was our guide, our evangelist, who revealed to us, in a succession of astounding lightning flashes, the entire expanse of the Modern World" (p. 121), and obviously they accepted any poetry which he put before them.

William Empson was another of Richards' students, and in his *Seven Types of Ambiguity* (1930) he made extensive use of Hopkins' poems, his critical method being influenced by Graves' and Miss Riding's "analysis of a Shakespeare Sonnet . . . in *A Survey.*" Empson quoted "Spring and Fall" as an example of the fourth "type" of ambiguity, in which "two or more meanings of a statement do not agree among themselves, but combine to make clear a more complicated state of mind in the author" (p. 168). Under the seventh "type," which "occurs when the two meanings of the word, the two values of the ambiguity, are the two opposite meanings defined by the context, so that the total effect is to show a fundamental division in the poet's mind" (p. 244), Empson stressed the importance of opposites in Freudian analysis and decided that such opposites in poetry mark "a centre of conflict." "The Windhover"—which he discussed at length—gives an "evident example of the use of poetry to convey an indecision, and its reverberation in the mind" (p. 284). Empson's analytical criticism, with its strong overtones of Freudian psychology, stands as a herald to a type of Hopkins criticism written extensively in the 1930s and still practiced today.

There were other notices of Hopkins in the 1920s of course, but they followed the orthodox tradition of criticism exemplified by earlier reviewers of the *Poems*. An informed essay was contributed to *America* (XXXIX [Oct. 6, 1928], 619-20) by G. F. Lahey, S.J., who saw that Hopkins' "admirers, unconsciously or no, have been biased by Bridges' necessarily distorted view of his life and religious ideals." Lahey realized, as did Miss Jessica North in her essay, "Quality in Madness" (*Poetry*, XXXIV [Aug., 1929], 270-73), that Hopkins had not been properly appreciated. Miss North's idea was that Hopkins had heard "inspired sounds . . . [which] came in a rush of magically associated words and phrases, arranged by instinct and not by reason, and so inevitably welded together." She proclaimed Hopkins a "modern" poet: he "was born too early to be one of the modernists of today. He would otherwise have been the master of them all."

· From these reviews, studies, and chance remarks there emerges a fairly definite picture of Hopkins' growing reputation. Knowledge of him was largely restricted to England where, although ignored by the general public, he was studied by the poets and poet-critics at Oxford (who took him as a model for their poetic practice) and by the non-orthodox critics at Cambridge (who used him as an example for their theories). Both groups discerned some of the qualities of the poems, but for the most part they interpreted Hopkins for their own ends. Yet because they used him, they caused his name to be known and interest in him to be awakened. The enthusiastic reception of the *Poems* in 1930 was thus largely due to the work of advanced critics and young poets, although it was also influenced by the new attitudes toward "difficult" poetry which were rapidly evolving. Nineteen-nineteen was one of the most propitious years in which Hopkins' poetry could have been brought before the public, since only in the 1920s was an appropriate criticism developed for it. The "appreciation" which his work would have met, had it been published before 1918, would probably have been of little help to the reader seeking to understand the poems; had the poems been published after the 1920s, critics would have applied their newly learned techniques to them with little sense of urgency or necessity. But published in 1918, they demanded the attention of readers confronted by the poetry of T. S. Eliot, the Sitwells, Cummings, and other experimental writers. Their poems demanded a new criticism, from which Hopkins benefitted. The understanding of his work has subsequently grown with the understanding of new ways of criticism, and his poems have become a part of twentieth-century literature. Because of this connection with the modern literary scene, it is only in the past two decades that Hopkins has been judged in relationship to his own time, and that a more just evaluation has been made of his work.

NOTES

1 This essay is a condensation (by the author) of the two articles, "Gerard Manley Hopkins and His Public, 1889-1918" and "The Reception of Gerard Manley Hopkins' *Poems,* 1918-30," *Modern Philology,* LVII (1959) and LXIII (1965). Copyright 1959 and 1965 the University of Chicago.

I have made extensive use of the bibliographies compiled by Sister Mary Patricia, C.S.J., *Bulletin of Bibliography,* XX (1950-53), 38-44, 63-67, and by Norman Weyand, S.J., *Immortal Diamond* (1949). I am also indebted to Mr. Gerard Hopkins and the O. U. P. for permission to examine at Amen House press clippings concerning the *Poems* (1918). Place of publication for all works cited is London, except where otherwise noted.

2 Information from a letter by Mrs. Abercrombie to Mr. Julian Trevelyan, Jan. 15, 1958, which was requested by the latter for the present writer.

3 Cited by Humphry House, *Notebooks of Gerard Manley Hopkins* (1937) , p. v.

4 Quoted by Fr. Keating in his review of *Letters of Gerard Manley Hopkins, Month,* CLXV (Feb., 1935), 128.

5 *Letters* (1935), p. xx.

6 *Loc. cit.,* n. 2.

7 Identified by Mr. Arthur Crook, assistant editor, in 1957. There are interesting similarities between Clutton-Brock's review and his essay, "The Fantastic School of English Poetry," *Cambridge Modern History* (1906), IV, 760-75.

8 The reviewer's approach was very much like that of Roger Fry, which was described to me by Mrs. Pamela Diamond (Fry's daughter) in 1958. "I do remember very clearly," she wrote, "about 1919 when the Hopkins poems first came out in a volume, my father's rapture, no other word will suffice. He read them aloud—better than I have ever heard them read—to all and sundry."

9 Identified by Miss Janet Smith, literary editor of the *New Statesman* in 1958.

10 A shortened version of this review was published in the *Freeman,* New York: VIII (Oct. 24, 1923), 156-7.

11 An expanded version of this essay with greater emphasis on Hopkins' "modernity" is in O'Neill's *Essays on Poetry* (Dublin, 1920).

12 Simon Nowell-Smith, "Bridges, Hopkins, and Dr. Daniel," *TLS,* (Dec. 13, 1957), p. 764.

13 The Editor of the *TLS,* considering Geoffrey Grigson's *Gerard Manley Hopkins* in the leader for March 18, 1955 (p. 165), remarked that "it was not till the publication of the second revised edition of [Hopkins'] poems in 1930, with the late Charles Williams's introduction, that he began to be widely read, and to become an active influence on

other poets." On April 29, 1955 (p. 209), Mr. Graves suggested in a letter "that what made Gerard Manley Hopkins 'an active influence' . . . may not have been the publication of a second revised edition of his poems . . . but a rapid exhaustion of the stagnant original edition: due to certain carefree paragraphs in *A Survey of Modernist Poetry* . . . which first described Hopkins as a modern." He also claimed that the *Survey* "launched Professor Empson, and by a chain-reaction the whole 'Cambridge School,' and finally half the English professors in the United States, on their similar explorations of Hopkins's other elliptical verses." But Professor Richards' essay in the *Dial* was published before *A Survey*.

SELECTIVE BIBLIOGRAPHY

Primary Sources

Hopkins, Gerard Manley. *Poems of Gerard Manley Hopkins*. Edited by W. H. Gardner. 3rd ed. London: Oxford University Press, 1948.

—————. *Poems and Prose of Gerard Manley Hopkins*. Edited by W. H. Gardner. London: Penguin Books, 1953.

—————. *A Hopkins Reader*. Edited by John Pick. Revised edition. Garden City, N.Y.: Image Books, 1966.

—————. *The Note-Books and Papers*. Edited by Humphry House. New York: Oxford University Press, 1937.

—————. *The Correspondence of Gerard Manley Hopkins and Richard Watson Dixon*. Edited by Claude Colleer Abbott. London: Oxford University Press, 1935.

—————. *Further Letters of Gerard Manley Hopkins including his Correspondence with Coventry Patmore*. Edited by Claude Colleer Abbott. 2nd ed. revised. London: Oxford University Press, 1956.

—————. *The Letters of Gerard Manley Hopkins to Robert Bridges*. Edited by Claude Colleer Abbott. London: Oxford University Press, 1935.

Secondary Sources

Boyle, Robert, S.J. *Metaphor in Hopkins*. Chapel Hill: University of North Carolina Press, 1960.

Gardner, W. H. *Gerard Manley Hopkins, 1844-1889*. 2 Vols. New Haven: Yale University Press, 1948-49.

Hartman, Geoffrey (Ed.), *Hopkins: A Collection of Critical Essays*. Englewood Cliffs, N. J. Prentice Hall, 1966.

Hill, Archibald A. "An Analysis of 'The Windhover.' An Experiment in Structural Method," *PMLA,* LXX (December, 1955), 968-78.

The Kenyon Critics (Ed.), *Gerard Manley Hopkins*. Norfolk, Conn.: New Directions, 1945.

Peters, W. A. M., S.J. *Gerard Manley Hopkins, A Critical Essay towards the Understanding of his Poetry*. London: Oxford University Press, 1948.

Pick, John. *Gerard Manley Hopkins: Priest and Poet*. 2nd ed. New York: Oxford University Press, 1966.

Schneider, Elizabeth W. "Sprung Rhythm: A Chapter in the Evolution of Nineteenth-Century Verse," *PMLA,* LXXX (June, 1965) 237-253.

——————. " 'The Wreck of the Deutschland': A New Reading," *PMLA,* LXXXI (March, 1966) 110-122.

Ward, Dennis. "Gerard Manley Hopkins's 'Spelt from Sibyl's Leaves,'" *The Month,* VIII, n.s. (July, 1952), 40-51.

Warren, Austin. *Rage for Order*. "Gerard Manley Hopkins." Chicago: University of Chicago Press, 1948.

Weyand, Norman, S.J. (Ed.), *Immortal Diamond: Studies in Gerard Manley Hopkins*. New York: Sheed and Ward, 1949.

CONTRIBUTORS

J. HILLIS MILLER is Professor and Chairman of the English Department at Johns Hopkins University, and is the author of: *Charles Dickens: The World of His Novels* (1958); *The Disappearance of God* (1963); and *Poets of Reality; Six Twentieth-Century Writers* (1965).

MRS. MARJORIE DOWNING is the Dean of Faculty at Scripps College, Claremont, California.

MAURICE B. MCNAMEE, S.J., is Professor and Chairman of the English Department at St. Louis University and is the author of *Honor and the Epic Hero* (1960).

WILLIAM D. TEMPLEMAN is Professor of English at the University of Southern California and is co-editor of *English Prose of the Victorian Era* (1938).

MARGARET STOBIE is Professor of English at St. John's College, University of Manitoba.

ELGIN W. MELLOWN is an Assistant Professor of English at Duke University.

CAROLYN SCOTT has been on the English faculty at the University of Kentucky, Washington University, and Fontbonne College.

JAMES SCOTT is Associate Professor of English at St. Louis University. His writings have appeared in *Philological Quarterly, Nineteenth Century Fiction, American Quarterly,* and the *Journal of Aesthetics and Art Criticism.*

CARMELITE MONASTERY
Beckley Hill
Barre, Vt., 05641

DATE BORROWED

_____